THE HURRICANE BOOK

a sailing captain's memoirs

D. RANDY WEST

ISBN-10: 1453845496
EAN-13: 9781453845493
LCCN: 2010914452

Acknowledgements

The most important people to thank in the writing of this book are all my friends who have lent a good ear to listen to some great stories. Every last one of them advised me to "Write it down!" As for illustration, Gail Rappley and Michelle Aulicino-Dery as well as Kevin and Michelle Schloot were kind enough to let me use their memorable photos to show just what a hurricane can do along with sailing shots of *Shadowfax*. I will forever be indebted to them. Kudos go as well to Weather Underground and NOAA for their hurricane tracking charts. After all, a picture IS worth a thousand words.

Author's note:

These storm stories are true. I experienced each and every one of them and lived to tell the tale. Please be aware that they are as I remember them. For persons involved in this book and who don't quite remember them in the same way or context as I have, never forget the immortal words of Harry Truman, "Goddamn eyewitnesses, always ruin a good story!"

map of Caribbean and the Bahamas

Hurricanes: an introduction

In the beginning a storm was a wonder, excitement, just a little scary, and they were few and far between. In the end a storm was more humbling, harrowing, frightening, and there were way too many for comfort. Up until now, eighteen storms in fifty-six years is not a good average, but such is life in the tropics.

At the start, I was just a little kid growing up in central Florida. The family had a town business, a farm in the country, a beach house, and I identified with all of them. I was a redneck, a surfer, a florist, a student, a diver, a fisherman. Who would have thought that I would end up a sailor and a Caribbean character? I have lived over half my life in the islands, starting with the Bahamas and continuing into the West Indies. And as a sailor…Well, at one time I was asked by a prospective employer to do up a resume. However, rather than spend pages on it, I put it this way:

SAILING EXPERIENCE:

7 SORC (Southern Ocean Racing Conference) Races, 3 Newport to Bermuda Races, 1 Daytona to Bermuda Race, 2 Chicago/Mac Races, 1 Queen's Cup, 1 Admiral's Cup, 1 Carlsberg 500, 2 Fort Lauderdale to Key West

Races, 2 Key West Race Weeks, 2 Abaco Race Weeks, 25 Heineken Regattas, 21 Antigua Sailing Weeks, 16 Classic Yacht Regattas, 15 Caribbean Offshore Races, 6 Transatlantic, 2 trans Meds, 2 Trans Pacifics, 20 Rolex Regattas, 10 BVI Spring Regattas, 7 Bucket Races, 11 Niologues, 1 Around Europe Race, 1 IOD Worlds, 2 Hobie Worlds, 4 Hobie Nationals, 1 Stiletto Nationals, 1 J 30 Nationals, 1 Worell 1000.

I have also sailed into and back out of the Great Lakes via canal and the St. Lawrence Seaway twice and transited the Panama Canal four times. I have averaged about eight thousand miles per year of voyaging, maybe more! One summer I sailed three thousand miles just in Lake Michigan.

In other words, I have seen some weather and all in all have tried to keep myself between the two latitudes of the tropics and, for the most part, I have. Of course the North Atlantic gave me its calling as well as the far reaches of the Med, but the tropics are where I have my roots. But I am getting ahead of myself. This is about hurricanes. Hurricanes are tropical and I have heard, as well as know, a lot about hurricanes.

I had heard that they are unpredictable. I know that the wind has to blow consistently over seventy-five miles per hour to be considered a hurricane. Before that threshold is reached they are first categorized as a depression with a corresponding number and then a tropical storm with forty-five mile-per-hour winds and given a name. When I was young they all had female names and some sexist jokes came out of that but then, after the advent of the "new age" of women's rights and all, somebody decided that the storms should be alternately named after males then females and so on. So much for tradition is what I say.

In days of old, hurricanes were unknowns. We have sailing stories of survivors of shipwrecks where the great explorers encountered tremendous storms at sea, resorting to chopping away the masts and rigging of their ships to survive. Why, even the triumphant British army after the burning of Washington, D.C., in 1813 was devastated on their withdrawal from the Virginia peninsula and thwarted in their conquest of Baltimore because of a hurricane that caused more casualties to the land army than the battle for Washington and held the navy at sea while the reeling American army built up the defenses at Baltimore and Fort McHenry.

Meteorologists claim that we need hurricanes. It has something to do with the heating of the sea then the cooling of the sea. Hot weather makes sandstorms in the Sahara that roar westward across the warm tropical waters of the southern Atlantic, for example. There they suck up evaporating seawater. It clings to the Sahara dust particles in the high atmosphere, slowly causing the dust to become more and more saturated and without the cooling effects of land, methodically condensing into naturally occurring low pressure systems, winding counterclockwise, wanting to dump that rain, intensifying in wind strength and power until sometimes, if one is unlucky, unleash their fury over one's head. That would be me.

Chapter 1

Child's Play

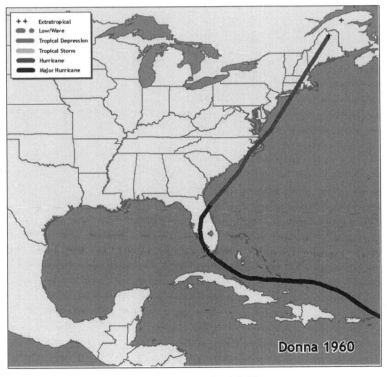

September 10, 1960
"Donna"

I had just been given a new army helmet and a Thompson .45-caliber sub machine gun...manufactured by Mattel, and the helmet was one of those plastic ones, olive drab in color with an accompanying chin strap and camo net. I was seven years old. It was the day after my birthday and we had been over in Daytona Beach, Florida, at the beach house. The weatherman had said that a real storm was threatening the state and coming across via the panhandle, somewhere near Apalachicola. I had never seen a "real" storm, but I was to get a taste of what a real storm meant.

Driving west from the beach to the country in DeLand took twenty minutes on the highway that my grandfather had built. He was quite the guy, Grandpa Grant Trundle. His age-old Georgia family had invented the bed by the Trundle name. His mom, my great-grandma, who had been accosted by Yankee cavalry during General Sherman's notorious "March to the Sea" during the American Civil War, had named his brother Lee out of respect for both sides of the Mason Dixon Line. Anyhow, Grandpa was the typical depression era farmer, wanting to do well for his family that included Grandma and two daughters. One was my aunt, of course, and the other my mom. He had moved to Florida during those years and worked as a superintendent and then owner of a rock mining and road building company that paved and built thoroughfares like U.S. 1, Alternate 27, and, yes, U.S. 17/92 from DeLand to Daytona Beach.

We arrived home via that road just about the time that the six o'clock news came on. The weatherman was announcing the coming storm on WESH TV... and the first image I saw when that TV came on was of the waves breaking through a beach house, our beach house! I had always liked waves.

I remember saying to my mother, "Mom, come look, there are waves crashing through the beach house." That was when Dad figured that taping up the windows wasn't good enough for the picture glass windows that were prominent on the DeLand house, and he broke out the plywood that was stored underneath for such occasions.

You see, according to Dad, the tape would give the windows extra strength against the wind and even hold them together in case they cracked. The plywood, however, was to prevent them from blowing out completely or, even worse, to stop flying debris from smashing through. He somehow knew that the storm was going to pass a little closer than the weatherman was thinking. My dad was born in Florida and my mom grew up there, but I was only seven years old and didn't know how many hurricanes they had seen in their lives, but Dad seemed to know what to do in the situation. With an older brother, a strong woman for a mother, and a native Floridian for a dad, I felt reassured.

Well, that storm arrived with a vengeance. She had been named Donna and she had already cut a swath through the West Indies with winds to 130 knots (that is 149.5 mph), destroying the fishing fleets of the time as well as house and home. On the island where I now live, St. Barth, a French island in the Caribbean, the entire fishing and trading fleet was washed ashore or sunk and the water came up so high that the dead floated out of their graves. The storm proved the death knell to the sailing, fishing, and cargo fleet of the island and brought in the age of diesel and gasoline-powered vessels. Passing over and wrecking the Florida Keys and then charging into the Gulf of Mexico, this monster looked to go into the Florida panhandle when she made the predictable unpredictable maneuver and, hanging a right, slammed into west Florida somewhere just south of Tampa.

From there Hurricane Donna roared across the state and my head. It rained buckets, the wind howled and shrieked. We were all camped out in the living room with us kids by the fireplace, the very center of the house. My little sister Sandy, as curious as always, had gotten up and was standing in front of the TV watching the news when the lightning started booming. I remember a flash bang and electricity jumping out of that tube and it seemed to engulf her in a green glow. As they say, curiosity killed the cat! It must have been static electricity, kind of like St. Elmo's fire, for it didn't harm her but scared the shit out of all of us! She ran back to the comfort of the quilt my brother and I had pulled over the top of our heads.

There was a huge bang a bit later when the small attic window blew out from the fury of the wind or flying debris, we couldn't discern which. It was midnight and Dad, followed by my big brother Jim, always the leader in crisis, and I ran upstairs to rectify the situation. Dad tried to nail a piece of plywood over the gaping hole as his hair flew. Jim yelled directions because it was loud up there and he felt someone needed directions, and I was silent in wonder.

We fixed that broken window and clambered back downstairs and under the quilt. What seemed not a long time after, however, it got very calm, and we ventured out the front door following Dad to investigate the quiet. Why, the sky was clear, stars were shining, and a mellow breeze was blowing through the neighborhood. My young self thought that was it then, storm gone; but Dad, being an old navy man and a Florida cracker to boot, knew that it was just the eye of the storm and that the wind would return in the opposite direction with the same fury as before. I didn't believe him at first, but goodness gracious, the howling started again, the power went out, and we endured until first light.

The storm abated then by what the weatherman called "moving safely out to sea." I always wondered if the men at sea saw it that way. We once again ventured out. I wore my new helmet, carried my plastic Thompson sub machine gun with aplomb, and stomped around like my comic book hero, Sergeant Rock, protecting the family from thieves and villains that I thought would materialize after the blow. But that didn't happen. Instead all the folk in the neighborhood got together and started to clean up the mess. Why, all the old towering oaks were down everywhere, the roads were blocked, and no one could move, so the men got out the chainsaws and axes and started busting up the oaks into firewood.

There was no power and nobody went to work—or school. I liked that part. We just all pitched in and cleaned up the mess, and what a mess it was. You could not venture far as the power lines tended to spark and jump around a lot and that was dangerous. And with no power we couldn't open the Frigidaire as it was vacuum-sealed, and by opening it you would let out all the cold air and the food would spoil. We were going to have to eat that later. So we subsisted a couple of days on canned food and stuff from the basement until ice became available, and then we opened the fridge. Boy was that first taste of cold milk a reward! And that, my friends, was some storm…only the first.

An interesting sideline and perhaps an explanation to the predictable unpredictability of the storm was that, in 1959, the state of Florida had purchased a right of way for the building of Interstate 4 over land, which included the "Field of the Dead." This was a parcel of land adjacent to Lake Munroe in Sanford, a town about eighteen miles south of DeLand.

It seems that in 1887, four members of a Catholic German pioneer family who had come to Mr. Sanford's colony on the shores of Lake Monroe to escape religious persecution in Protestant Germany had died during the yellow fever epidemic and had been buried in a field near the lake. Four wooden headstones marked the graves, as did an encircling barbed wire fence. Legend has it that in 1905, when the owner of the property tried to remove the headboards, his house burned down and his wife had him replace the markers. After the land was sold, the next owner tried to remove the barbed wire enclosure and his house too burned down. That was the start of "The Legend of the Field of the Dead."

In September 1960, during the survey for the right-of-way, the four marked but nameless graves were earmarked for relocation. However, the bureaucracy that prevailed forgot about this, and on September 9, the day that Donna was forecast to head into the panhandle or into Alabama, fill dirt was dumped over the graves. The storm then made an abrupt right turn toward Tampa, and oddly enough, the eye of the storm followed the route of the soon to be built I-4 starting just south of Tampa and ending in Daytona Beach. The destruction caused a delay of a month in the opening of the highway. The eye of Donna passed directly over the gravesite in the field beside Lake Monroe at midnight on September 10, the exact time our attic window blew out! Now tell me that is not weird!

Beach houses on a Florida beach after the passing of Hurricane Donna, 1960

Chapter 2

We Thought Hawaii Had Surf

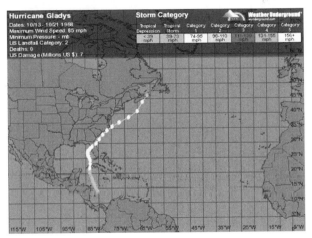

"Gladys"
October 18, 1968

Eight years went by before I saw my next real storm. I was fifteen years of age and attending DeLand Junior High School. My brother was a junior at DeLand High and he and all his friends had cars! My little sister was under my wing at DJHS following my footsteps, playing drums in the marching band. My second storm, Hurricane Gladys, was in the Gulf of Mexico, and off to Alabama she went, much like Donna in 1960. She then too took an abrupt right-hand turn and came ashore above Tampa near Cedar Key, blowing about one hundred miles per hour. That must have beat those Cedar Keyans up a bit along with their shrimp boat fleet, but by the time it passed south of Ocala, which in DeLand was where we lived, there wasn't much to it, just a bit of rain, thunder, lightening, and wind, lots of wind. By the fifteenth, the storm had gone on "safely out to sea" as the weathermen continued to muse. Gladys was off again skirting the eastern seaboard and then into the wide Atlantic.

Now I had been surfing since 1963 and pretty much had it down by '68. It is not as if we began to surf just like that. In the beginning there were few surfboards or even surfers. There were a few old men in Daytona Beach like Richard Albery the attorney or the lifeguard, sailor, pilot, and pier builder Gaulden Reed who had been at it since the 1920s. Gaulden even invented and rented canvas-covered floats that our parents got for us so we could ride waves in on our stomachs. That is the reason that as a child I loved waves so much.

Later, with the advent of foam boards manufactured by Hansen in Cardiff, California, or Miller and Daytona Beach Surf Shop, we started riding long boards. They were from nine to ten feet long and took two of us to carry to the beach. My first one was a used 9'10" Hansen and I still have it today, and my second, a collector's piece, is a 9'8" Daytona Beach Something Special by Miller and is hanging on the wall in my house. By 1968, we were riding short boards, mine being a Hansen super lite at 7'6". And as a young man, I had no fear. Young man, hah! It was the older boys, the friends of my brother, who had cars and no fear. Gus (who is dead now), Octavio, or my cousin Cliff would take me for a surf trip over to New Smyrna or Daytona or Ormond Beach to ride waves.

When Hurricane Gladys went off to sea she sure kicked up a huge swell, so Octavio took his younger brother, Norman, and me over to Ormond Beach to ride the waves at the pier that Gaulden had built after World War II. Octavio had just bought a brand-new Surfboards America surfboard at the Surfboards Galore Surf Shop in Daytona and wanted to test it out. Boy, the waves were huge and there was no paddling out through them so... we decide to run and jump off the end of the pier. We did just that...run and jump! It was about twenty feet to the water, and oh what a thrill. Then we'd catch whatever big wave came along first or else we'd get cleaned up and washed ashore. We'd ride that wave all the way to the beach, then run back up to the pier, out to the end, and off again. We were kings, invincible, and fearless... That's when the big waves came along!

The set of waves were so big that we all about got washed off the pier. I mean, here we were twenty feet off the water and this wave was breaking above us and about fifty yards farther out. Imagine five feet of white water rolling down the pier at you. Water was spurting up between the boards of the pier and over the railings. You had to just hang on to anything stable around you as the water washed over...and I mean HANG ON! After it has done its breaking—get this—the pier from us to the shore had washed away all together. We HAD to jump off then...And that's when I found God. I hit the water and came up to a wave twice as big as anything I had ever seen breaking. I got pounded so hard that I hit the bottom, and it is deep out there. Luckily it was a sand bottom, no rocks or coral, but it sure knocked the breath out of me. Now I could not find my way up or down but was just in this endless swirl and tug, a true maelstrom. I thought to myself, *that is it, game shut* when, just like that, I reached the surface in time to gasp a lung full of air as the next wave again pounded my ass to the bottom.

Now a youth can hold his breath a while, and a while longer when he has to, but in the end I just gave up. I could not find up or down, I panicked, and swam into the bottom. I then relaxed a second to gather my wits, and in my brain I told myself *this is it, one big inhale and my lungs are going to be just full of water and I am going to be dead, dead, dead.* It was kind of a peaceful realization, but I asked myself *do I really want to give it all up?* I thought, *oh what the hell, one final go at it and then the jig is up.* So I gave one last Herculean pull of the arms and, whoosh, sucked in all that seawater...which was all AIR! I was never so happy to be alive in my life, said my prayers of thanks right then and there, and allowed myself to be washed ashore. That was the end of surfing that day, and from the pictures I have since seen of Hawaii...I thought they had big waves!

Chapter 3

Guaranteed For Life

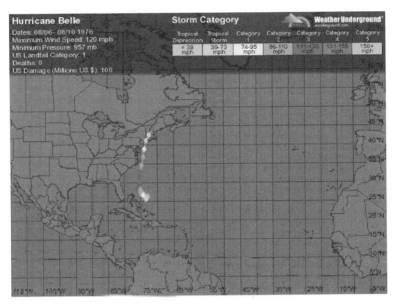

Hurricane Belle			Storm Category							Weather Underground
Dates: 08/06 - 08/10 1976			Tropical Depression	Tropical Storm	Category 1	Category 2	Category 3	Category 4	Category 5	
Maximum Wind Speed: 120 mph			< 39 mph	39-73 mph	74-95 mph	96-110 mph	111-130 mph	131-155 mph	156+ mph	
Minimum Pressure: 957 mb										
US Landfall Category: 1										
Deaths: 0										
US Damage (Millions US $): 100										

August 8, 1976
"Belle"

The year 1976 was an interesting year. My big brother was out of college and on his own, my little sister out of the house and...MARRIED! The big DeLand house was sold and gone and the parents had moved into a classy townhouse near the town center. I was back at school after two years of education and two years of touring the world. It had snowed in Florida and the Bahamas. I went on my first sailboat and sailing adventure, motoring in a twenty-eight-foot sloop from Hatchet Bay to Gregorytown in Eleuthera, Bahamas, a trip of eleven miles. Back home in Florida, my third storm appeared on the horizon. Belle was her name. She came up outside the Bahamas looking similar to all the rest...105 mph, circular rotation with a defined eye.

From June to November in my part of the world these storms regularly form off the west coast of Africa starting as what was later called a "tropical wave." Sometimes that would be it or, as I mentioned earlier, they would form into first a depression, then a tropical storm earning a name, and then when the wind became sustained at or over seventy-five miles per hour, a hurricane. However, this storm formed late and never touched land, thus no big deal is what I thought. After all, I had already weathered two storms. "Not much punch," we seasoned hurricane aficionados would say. But what the hey, I was still young, just finishing school at the University of South Florida, and spending more time at the beach than I did in class. Shoot, even though I was earning three degrees, I still had planned my days at school from Monday night to Friday morning allowing me to get to the beach every Friday before lunch and returning by Monday afternoon. I had no transportation, but with the beach house at my disposal, it was easy to invite anyone with wheels to the ocean for the weekend or, if that failed, I would jump out on the interstate, surfboard and bag in hand with a sign that said simply "the coast." That and a thumb accompanied by my gift of gab got me to the surf and back quick enough.

They (whomever "they" were) eventually came up with the idea of a neoprene leash for our surfboards. One end was attached to a loop of fiberglass built into the tail of the board while the other was secured to the surfer's ankle. That way when we fell—or "wiped out" in surfer lingo—we didn't have to suffer the long swim to shore to retrieve our boards. We had tried surgical tubing with a string inside of it tied to our fins, but that did not work. They either broke from not having enough elasticity or pulled the fin out of the board. However, the neoprene had ten times the elasticity, was incredibly stronger, and above all, guaranteed for life.

With that, we each bought one at West Wind Surf Shop in South Daytona. One must explain that Hurricane Belle had decided to pass us up, later to flail Long Island, Connecticut, Massachusetts, and finally New Hampshire before moving into the Canadian Maritimes, but passing close enough to Florida to send us incredible surf! Off we went to Daytona Beach so that we could ride waves at Sunglow Pier, new leashes and all.

We jumped off of that pier just as we had during Hurricane Gladys in 1968. We got to jump only once, however, because the owner was a fisherman and didn't like us surfers all that much; thus he closed the pier to our kind. Tommy, my friend since kindergarten, was with me riding the Nicols' gun he had brought back from Hawaii, and I had a new 7'2" pintail made by Natural Art Surfboards expressly for big waves like these that the storm had created.

Tommy and I rode some great waves. The current was so strong that we got swept down the beach about two miles riding wave after wave. We'd chat with the occasional surfer who managed to paddle out through the waves, grab a wave out of an approaching set, kick out before getting hammered, and paddle out again to start the sequence all over. As surf life would have it, we eventually got caught inside or made that one wipeout that ended the day as our leashes lasted all of two seconds in those tumbles!

We both washed ashore near each other and started our two-mile walk back to the car. Waves were huge and even at low tide there was not much beach to walk on. But the leashes! They were everywhere. The beach was littered with them, a testament to all who had tried to paddle out through the surf that day and either didn't make it or, like us, took that one fateful wipeout. All I could think about was just how much money did Rick from West Wind lose that day on his "Guaranteed for Life" neoprene leashes?

Chapter 4

He Huffed and He Puffed and He Blew the House Down

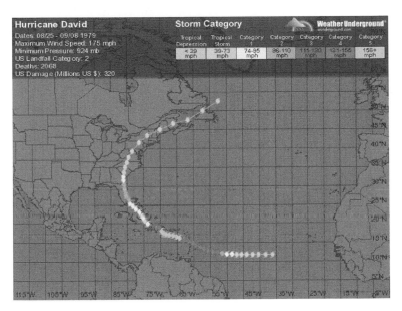

Hurricane David

Dates: 08/25 - 09/08 1979
Maximum Wind Speed: 175 mph
Minimum Pressure: 924 mb
US Landfall Category: 2
Deaths: 2068
US Damage (Millions US $): 320

Storm Category

Tropical Depression	Tropical Storm	Category 1	Category 2	Category 3	Category 4	Category 5
< 39 mph	39-73 mph	74-95 mph	96-110 mph	111-130 mph	131-155 mph	158+ mph

Weather Underground

September 3, 1979
"David"

By the end of the 1970s I had spent four years sailing catamarans sponsored by the local Florida suntan oil company Hawaiian Tropic. In fact, we were the only sponsored sailors in America. Ever since I had seen the *National Geographic* map of the Caribbean accompanying the adventures of the sailing yacht *Yankee* in the Antilles in 1965 I had wanted to learn how to sail and spend the rest of my life surfing those unexplored islands of the Spanish Main. Being a country surfer/redneck, those opportunities very rarely showed themselves. However, as Lady Luck would have it, in my last year of university I met Annie, now one of the greatest American sailors in the world. At our first encounter I asked her if she had a car and, if she did, would she like to go to my beach house for the weekend. The car was an affirmative and it came with a Hobie 16 attached! What luck!!! What a start. We surfed, we sailed—well, tried to sail—but there was no wind and the surf was huge! We surfed. We put off sailing until the following weekend.

The following weekend was the Hobie Midwinters Regatta on the west coast of Florida on Longboat Key, which Annie entered as the only woman skipper among 165 boats and me as crew…we finished fifth. (I still have the trophy.) Then came Christmas break and we sailed her Hobie from Coconut Grove, and the Coral Reef Yacht Club near Miami, to Key West on the outside. What an adventure and introduction to sailing. We observed nesting bald eagles on Elliot Key and camped at "Dynamite Docks" in Pennekamp Park. We

BBQed steaks on deserted Dove Key. We sailed into Key West and hung out with "Groovy" Gray, the Hobie Cat renter, and a country/folk guitar player named Jimmy. But to be honest, I really had no idea what I was doing; I just followed orders well. And as luck would have it, I met a man during the winter session just in chatting as I tended to do, and he enquired as to what I was going to do after college. I was graduating that quarter with three degrees after all.

I informed him that all I wanted to do was to learn to sail and go surfing in the West Indies. Impressed, he invited me to sail on his forty-foot two-tonner called *Imp*, which was located at the St. Petersburg Yacht Club. Two weekends of that and I was the guy on the rail asking the fellow next to me when the race would start... to which he would answer, "Twenty minutes ago!" Was I lost or what?

After graduation I applied as a graphic artist to Hawaiian Tropic, a local company in Daytona Beach. They, however, had no openings in the advertising department, but as rumor would have it they had heard that I had sailed well in the Hobie Midwinters and also crewed on *Imp*, which at the time was the boat with the most wins in the world, and so they asked if they could sponsor me to race catamarans. You see, their trademark happened to be a Hobie 16 jumping waves. I still had no idea how to sail but didn't let THAT stop me...I agreed to the sponsorship. So we spent all week riding waves with our Hobie 16s off the beaches in Daytona and New Smyrna and every other weekend at a regatta. If it was flat during the week, thank God our mentor, the famous Gaulden Reed, would show up with his Hobie 18, set up a race course of buoys, and off we would go round and round until we got it right! Timed starts, jibe marks, beats to weather, the rules, all of that sailing stuff and jargon we had to get right. I learned my lesson well and by 1979 was winning regattas and riding any size wave in any wind on my Hobie 16.

What a great job, although it lasted only the season (March to October). It paid the bills, kept me in great shape, and allowed me to spend the winter in the Caribbean as a skipper of a private yacht. I kept a little house on the beach in New Smyrna Beach year-round called "Sandy Shack," and that became our redoubt when Hurricane David decided to tumble along the coastline.

This storm had come out of the eastern Atlantic Ocean as most do and wailed on the island nation of Dominica, destroying shipping, the banana crop that was its main staple, and most everything else with winds up to 125 knots (143.75 mph). Today there are still beached and sunken ships in the harbor of Portsmouth left behind by David. The Dominican Republic was next to be slammed as winds topped 150 knots (that is 172.5 mph!). Then, luckily for everyone else, the mountains of that island beat the storm down to a minimal threat at eighty knots as it swept through the Bahamas, finally making landfall at West Palm Beach, Florida. Winds oscillated between seventy and eighty knots as it wound up the coast to go offshore at New Smyrna, somewhere in the vicinity of the Sandy Shack.

That weekend there had been a pro surfing contest located at Cocoa Beach, about forty-five miles south of New Smyrna Beach, and we had taken two of the Hawaiian Tropic boats down there to advertise for the sponsor. With the storm threatening, we loaded up the van and truck with the gear, two pro surfers—Alan and J., both from California—and headed home. By the time we got there, the waves had gotten GIANT! We took the two 16s down the beach to Bethune. This used to be, in the '60s, the "separate but equal" beach south of New Smyrna. We figured that it was far enough from town that we would not be interfered with by the local authority for launching into such formidable surf. We were wrong.

You should have seen the looks on the faces of the beach patrol when they came to stop us! "You guys! What the hell do you think you are doing?" they shouted over the wind, for it was sure howling by now, the storm being in Palm Beach and all. "You are FORBIDDEN to go out there," they said. Well, we gave them the old "sure we can, watch us," to which they informed us they were not going to come out to save us. What the heck...we were young.

Then along came the U.S. COAST GUARD in the biggest pickup truck I had ever seen, flashing lights, siren, and all. This bug-eyed guy, looking like a chief because of his hat, jumped out demanding that we "cease and desist!" We launched anyway...into the biggest waves we have ever ridden...ever. And it was howling. Probably twenty-five to thirty-five knots of wind, so we put four guys on each boat; two on the trapeze just to hold those 16s down. Outside the surf line the troughs were so deep between the waves that all one could see was the "16" emblem on the sail and the masthead, and that emblem is way up there.

We pulled off some unbelievable cutbacks and off-the-lips riding those monsters. As the tide grew higher we would fly down the beach in the last bit of shore break in two feet of water, flying a hull, still with four guys on the boat. That was something; stupid, yes, but really, really something!

As David would have it, he decided to get closer and we decide to hightail it back to the humble abode, stopping first at a hurricane party at David Donovan's house until a tree fell through and into the screened-in swimming pool. Then it was off to Sandy Shack as the rest of the revelers headed across the bridge to higher ground.

Now you have to understand that Sandy Shack was the first house built on the beach way back in 1900. It was built on stilts twenty feet in the air and you could not see the surf from the house because of the dunes, as the ole folks told me. By 1945, when someone added an "L"-shaped screened-in porch, the sand had built up to floor level but high tide was right outside the door. By 1979 the sand had built back two sets of dunes. The shack was a split-level thing with a bedroom and bath upstairs and a small window in the bath that looked down on the eaves of the roof. That became important when the storm arrived.

Because it blew stink! It blew dogs off chains! Eighty knots of wind coming off of the sea carries a lot of spray and spume and we could not see out the front or the back of the house. It was just white. But out of that window you could see through the lee created by the eaves of the roof a small way behind the house to where my Hobie cat was tied to its trailer. Well, it was flying! All the attachments were blowing off the roof, and below that, my Hobie was getting airborne with every puff then slamming back to earth. What a sight!

I called a friend who lived across the bridge and asked if I could bring the boat over and put it in her garage, to which she agreed. But as we hurriedly drove out onto the street we realized that with all the stunts the trailer had been pulling off while flying, it had broken its axle. So we dragged the thing down the road to the neighbor's house that had two stout trees beside it and lashed the boat and trailer to them. Hah! In the end the trees were gone but the Hobie survived.

On the way back to the shack the police stopped us and informed the crew and me that it was time to evacuate the island. We told them we were just running back to the house to get my little brother and then we would skedaddle on across the bridge. The crew did leave, there never was any little brother, and just my roommate, Tom, my girlfriend, and I remained to weather the storm.

And it blew pretty darn hard first one way and then the other. The power remained on the whole time and we watched the storm pass on TV. Thank God the worst of it hit at low tide as the waves came up to the house anyway. Oh, it got bad; it was a storm after all. The sliding glass window was bowing in so much from the wind that we nailed two-by-fours across the jamb to keep it from blowing in. The house seemed to move a little so we knocked together a frame with two-by-fours—inside the house! That helped shore the old Sandy Shack right up. And the storm moved safely out to sea.

The next day when the bridges were let down, we were the only ones on the whole island heading across to the mainland. We were off to Ponce Inlet on the north side of the jetty to surf! We zoomed passed the long lines of all our neighbors as they were heading back to the island to see what remained as we, in boyish glee, having been survivors, would be the first into the surf. And what of Sandy Shack, you might ask?

Well, the humble abode had a bit of a slant to it, so much in fact that they (whomever they were) decided to condemn it. And that was a shame because the shack was the first house on the beach and I had to move out in two days, store all my belongings at my parents' flower shop in DeLand, Florida, and head on down to Antigua, in the British West Indies, a bit early that year and live on the sailing yacht *Tranquility*.

The island nation of Dominica after the destruction left
by Hurricane David, 1979
Courtesy National Geographic

Chapter 5

And the Storm Moved Safely Out to Sea

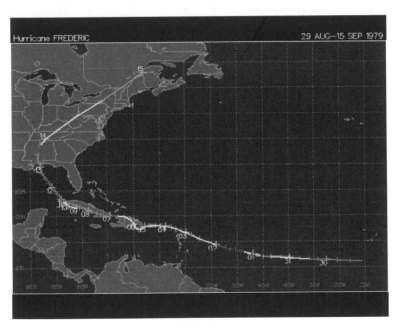

Hurricane FREDERIC   29 AUG–15 SEP 1979

September 7, 1979
"Frederic"

Tranquility was a fifty-two-foot custom ketch designed by Charles Mason, owned by Sam Bass with family, and was my home away from home in the winters of my "Hawaiian Tropic" years. I had met Sam and family while they were passing through Daytona Beach, Florida, and I was sailing Hobie cats and a Stiletto twenty-seven-foot cat for my sponsor, Hawaiian Tropic suntan lotions and oils. Although sponsored, we could just make ends meet, and me being an artist with three degrees from the University of South Florida meant I would use my extraordinary skills and sign paint for a few bucks on the side. Thus I painted *Tranquility* on the transom of Sam's new boat, and he confided in me that he did not know how to sail and would I teach him and family as we toured south to the West Indies.

As a matter of fact, he had been sailing down the Chesapeake Bay when he got caught up in a passing front. The wind had filled in from behind with such a fury that he could not get his sails down, and all of them were up! One could have cut the halyards and the sails would not have come down, ensnared in the power of the wind as they were. But as God does look after children, drunks, and sailors, to Sam's good fortune the U.S. Navy fleet out of Norfolk, Virginia, was approaching as Sam was exiting the bay entrance and blowing by the stern of the carrier *USS Saratoga*. *Tranquility* was caught in the lee created by the massive ship, narrowly missing a collision, allowing Sam to dump the sails...and motor all the way to Florida!

Would I teach him and his family??? Yes was the answer. I then spent three winters with them sailing to South America and back to the Lesser Antilles where we were based out of Montserrat, a speck of a British colony near Antigua. And it was here in Antigua that I would meet the boat only four days after weathering David and losing my house in New Smyrna Beach.

Sam was an interesting character to say the least! Just so that you would remember his name he would tell you that he "was named after the outlaw Sam Bass." He had been on submarines in the U.S. Navy during World War II and had rejoined the armed services; the U.S. Air Force this time as a navigator on bombers over Korea. After that war, he had started an electronics engineering business following getting his degree at Princeton. That was when the U.S. government gave him his third calling. He was to report to a man named Oppenheimer and go to work on a project so secret that Dr. Oppenheimer didn't even know what they were doing. As it turned out, the project was the nuclear submarine *Nautilus,* and Sam's job was to figure out how to shoot rockets off the damned thing.

Sam had wanted to revisit St. Thomas, the American Virgin Island where he had been stationed during the war and also been dock master in 1977 at a marina called Yacht Haven. I was all for it because we would be there for my birthday on the ninth and I had great local friends that I would love to visit like the immigrated St. Barth families who lived on North Side as well as Hull Bay, a great surf spot. We set out immediately for the VI. Upon my arrival, I remember the wind being a bit northerly so it was a very nice reach to start. The trip would be all night, all day, and with Sam, Cathy, and me standing watches, it promised to be a no-brainer; an easy slide up the islands passing St. Barth, St. Maarten/St. Martin, and Anguilla before crossing the Anegada Passage to the Virgin Islands.

Well, the weather turned to shit. The northerly built into a blow, then a gale. We were reaching along under reefed mizzen and staysail quite nicely and Sam was on his old hobby, the ham radio, chatting with friends around the world. Matter of fact, it was Sam who had contacted me the day after Hurricane David by what is called a phone patch via his ham to ask if I could come down early and sail up to the Virgin Islands with the family. It seemed that he was in contact with a ham operator in New Mexico who was in turn in contact with a ham operator in Jacksonville, Florida, who in turned called me on the phone, and through this method I was able to talk with Sam. Seeing as I had a crooked house, well, what the heck? I signed on. And the "Ham Net" was the weather in those days. Oh, we had Saba Radio on top of the Dutch island of Saba, but a few days earlier my friend David had passed, blowing away their antennae.

So on the ham was when we first heard about the next storm...Frederic formed at sea and was now at the coordinates at approximately 17.5 north, 59 west...or to say, right where we were located, and no wonder the weather was so bad! This was to be my first, but far from my last, storm at sea. The book...believe me, we read the book then, which said to put the wind on the starboard quarter and run with it, and that is exactly what we did. Waves got huge but not scary as we had expected. It blew white, but it was at night so we never really saw how bad it was. We thank the Lord for small favors.

The following day we were scudding along under a triple reefed mizzen and staysail when we chanced upon the small island of Culebra, one of the "Spanish Virgins" belonging to the Puerto Rican group. There we zoomed in for shelter from the storm at Ensenada Honda and unleashed all of our four anchors and let the storm abate. Abating meant to set an anchor watch, check the lines for chafe. Sticking your head out now and again to make sure no one was dragging down upon you was a good call. There were a few boats in the anchorage, after all. Keeping the kids interested was one of my jobs, so games, cards, and yes, even cooking kept them enthralled. Luckily it was a mere blow inside Ensenada Honda, quite comfortable and no danger. Frederic went on to intensify and smash up Haiti; we had a small birthday party for me, spent a day in St. Thomas, and headed home to Montserrat.

They said that Frederic was a minimal hurricane and never blew more than seventy-five knots as it passed St. Maarten, but it seemed a lot windier than that to me. When we sailed back by St. Maarten on the way home, well, it didn't seem minimal to them either. The island looked as if someone had taken a red paintbrush to everything. There was not a leaf, just this red hue. And the water! Water was everywhere. The Great Salt Pond went from sea to the drive-in theater. You could actually dinghy across town to where the drive-in theater used to be. The screen was said to be somewhere near San Juan, Puerto Rico, but I never saw it blow by.

I had visited St. Maarten/St. Martin in 1977 for the launching of a seventy-five-foot catamaran named *Ppalu* and visited the two hospitals there looking for medical care so I had an idea of what the island looked like before a storm. But this! There was water everywhere, water and mud, and dead animals and more mud and water. I, to this day, cannot believe that not a single person was killed. And I remember saying to Sam in the height of the storm at sea the old adage "It must be hell ashore on a night like this!" For the first time too I realized what the weatherman meant when he said that "The storm has moved safely out to sea."

Chapter 6

Aloha Na Kaoi

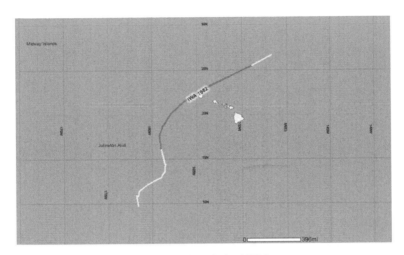

November 24, 1982
"Iwa"

By the end of the '70s I found myself living on the French side of the island of St. Martin, sailing small groups of tourist over to my favorite island of St. Barth for the day and returning at night. All day in St. Barth, all night in St. Martin, and every weekend in St. Barth gave me a taste and love of the French. I savored the food, learned the language, both French and French Creole, the island lingo. I taught the kids to surf and sail, received two free kisses from all the women—a custom I have come to adore. I was a bon vivant. Vive la France, I loved my life…and then Mitterrand, the damn communist, was elected president of France. That meant that all the French francs I had been stashing away in the French banks were going to devalue to nothing. I had to do something.

I chose to leave, but where? I asked. Florida was too hot in the summer, too cold in the winter. California had waves with Eskimo-related water temperatures. But Hawaii was an option. I loved island living, Hawaii was American, and what the heck, I could probably learn pidgin, another local lingo, once I had "immigrated." Surfing there was the best in the world, and hey, that was where catamarans came from, right? I was sure to get a job.

A story in itself is my trip to Hawaii, but suffice to say I arrived safely. After a few trials and tribulations, employment came along as a skipper of a sixty-foot catamaran, vintage 1957. Housing was to be found on the North Shore during the winter at the surf break called Pipeline and in the summer on board a forty-two-foot sport fisherman in the Kewalo Yacht Basin, Honolulu. I could write a book just on my adventures in Hawaii alone, but this is about hurricanes and Hawaii had not had a storm in thirty-five years. "Iwa" was to be a story maker!

The weatherman had mentioned a storm out in the Pacific somewhere south of the islands. Rather than take the bus out to the North Shore as I normally did as the winter season was upon us, I opted to stay in town for the upcoming swell generated by the storm. It started blowing Kona; that is, the wind was coming out of the south-southwest and the sea began to rise up. That would make perfect windsurfing conditions so I, with two friends, Roger and Joey, launched from the beach at the Ali Wai Yacht Basin. We would scream outside all the way to the spot called "Fours," which is almost to the Diamond Head sea buoy jibe, and ride waves all the way back to the Ali Wai. Waves were ten feet, the wind was side shore and howling, and we played till dark. Talk about fun, we were the *alii*, the kings, and could do no wrong.

I decided to stay the night on the sport fisher. They had a charter the next day and would be leaving the dock at seven o'clock in the morning. Thus I would be off the boat first thing and into wind surfing heaven. But nooo! I may not be a Kama'aina, or native born, but perhaps more like a white West Indian. When I stuck my head out of that boat in the morning and took one look at the sky, I said to myself, "Shit! Shit! Shit! This storm is coming here...And it is coming here TODAY!"

Now the captain of the sport fisherman *was* a Kama'aina and he showed up for the charter. Well, I had already triple tied the boat and was taking off the Bimini top before the wind did when he started screaming about the charter and taking the boat out and that I know nothing, and it was just blowing Kona, and Hawaiians would go out in anything. He had never seen a real storm before.

We were about to come to blows when the owner of the company showed up in a real panic yelling something about a storm that was coming called Iwa. All the big boats started leaving by then to get to a safer harbor. That would be Kehee Lagoon beside the airport or onto the ship docks in the Port of Honolulu. Seas were up to fifteen feet by now and it was blowing out of the south-southwest at forty knots. The 146-foot *Invader*, a Herreshoff schooner, pulled out of her slip to head to Kehee, and the waves were so steep at the entrance to Kewalos that both her props come out of the water as she pitched over them.

We also knew we were in serious trouble when we saw the fleet at Pearl Harbor head to sea. Aircraft carriers, guided missile cruisers, destroyers, fast frigates… all were making a beeline for the open sea. The last ship out, a fast frigate, had to punch through twenty-foot breaking waves. One seaman on the anchor watch at the bow of the ship was killed when he got washed down the deck and onto a stanchion; the others had broken bones. One of them had the wherewithal to jump off the ship entirely and came through unscathed! Now this was a real storm!

With *Invader's* slip empty, we opted to move the sport fisherman in there as the slip was quite long, wide, and a safe place to spider-web the forty-two-foot boat into. Two slips down was my cat, *Paradise Cove*, which we lashed triple time to dock and moorings and I set up a command center there and then. The boss went off to Honolulu Harbor to take care of his ships, and the crew and I hunkered down to take on the storm.

And man did it start to blow. And things started to fly and these here Hawaiians had never seen a hurricane before. Damn if it didn't blow all night. The sea got so high that if we had not lashed those boats down triple tight they would have shot across the Ala Moana Blvd. right into Ruth's Steakhouse! Just like clockwork, at four in the morning (it is always at four o'clock in the morning), a floating dock broke loose with two sport fishermen attached and commenced to blow away. The crews, of course, were in awe. No one had ever seen anything like this before. Well, off it all went, down the yacht basin heading for yours truly. So I grabbed a long rope, tied it around my waist, and swam out to the vagrant raft up. Climbing on board the dock I quickly attach the rope to a piling so that the boys could pull it back in and make it fast. I must have been nuts!

By first light Iwa had let us be and gone on to wreck the island of Kauai. It's not that we were not wrecked too. All the power lines were down. All the underground parking lots under all the beachside hotels were full of seawater and sand and, of course, cars. I always wondered what happened to all those rental cars after they were towed out and shipped off the island... maybe Kansas and a fire sale. Who knows? The Wainai side of the island, which is the west side and traditionally where the Hawaiians live, really got hit hard with many an islander's roof amiss, and no power, but the Hawaiians can live island style without any problem. It was the tourist who had problems coping. But we were ok. Shoot, my sixty-foot cat had charged so hard trying to get to Ruth's Steakhouse that her bottom was completely clean. I had never seen that. The yachts at the Ali Wai had a bit of a mash up. The North Shore was powerless and the grocery stores were giving away ice cream before it melted. We even learned how to make pizzas in a skillet over an open fire. The surf was gooooooooood and we were alive, thus we surfed and celebrated Thanksgiving in more ways than one.

Did Anyone Say Anything About a Storm?

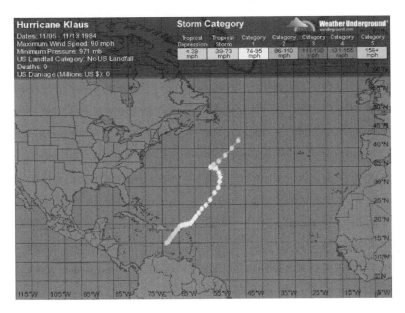

November 7–8, 1984
"Klaus"

I don't think that Hawaii had another hurricane for ten more years, but I didn't wait around to find out. The Caribbean was truly in my heart, and after two years of "aloha no kaoi" this and "wa bra you pau already?" that, I ended my sojourn to the Pacific islands and returned to St. Barth. French Creole was an easier language anyway, the surf was uncrowded, and the catamarans were faster, prettier, and they paid me to race them!

Racing became my mainstay, and I found myself sailing in all the regattas locally as well as internationally. I skippered an array of boats from a sixty-eight-foot maxi cat to a forty-four-foot two-tonner, a thirty-six-foot Macgregor cat, and even a twenty-four-foot quarter-tonner. Having all these boats in my care sure kept my hands full and I didn't need another hurricane. Klaus was to be his name. I was living in the lagoon in St. Maarten aboard the S&S 44 *Blue Jennifer* at the time. We had unfortunately dismasted her during Antigua Sailing Week and had the boat by the rigging shop in St. Maarten for repairs. *Eagle*, the sixty-eight-foot Brookes cat, was on charter taking one person over to St. Barth, *Defiance*, the Macgregor thirty-six-foot cat, had also been dismasted during the Grand Prix of Martinique and was hauled out awaiting a new rig, and the twenty-four-foot Spronk quarter-tonner *Kitchema* was in the bay in Phillipsburg, St. Maarten, for the upcoming November 11 Regatta St. Maarten Day. It had rained for nine days.

That particular day I had lucked upon seeing a weather fax printed out from a visiting mega yacht, *Non Stop,* and had noticed a peculiar weather pattern had formed south of us near Curacao, a Dutch island off the coast of Venezuela. Although not mentioned in the morning weather forecast, the fax seemed to me to indicate that there would be a nice-sized swell generated by it, and waves on the south shore of St. Maarten were imminent. I grabbed my surfboard and drove over the island to Phillipsburg that very afternoon.

It was three o'clock when I crested the hill and notice a green squall coming from the direction of St. Barth. I remember worrying about the sixty-foot cat *El Tigre,* for she was in St. Barth with twenty tourists on board day tripping. I told myself that they would have to wait till that squall passed before they left because when you see green in a squall it means you will see very high and very dangerous wind speeds arriving in the gusts. Well, at three thirty *El Tigre* arrived, flying into the harbor with only a jib up. She had not waited for the squall to pass and had completed the thirteen-mile sail in exactly thirty minutes meaning she averaged twenty-six knots! Now that is flying for a sailboat. I mean, normally the cats that sail over to St. Barth arrive by five o'clock, and arriving by four thirty is a fast trip, but a three thirty arrival? All that I could say was "my goodness!"

I often wondered what *Eagle* would have done in that weather, but luckily she had returned early and was safe on the fuel dock when I arrived at the marina. The wind was picking up out of the south, so rather than go to her slip, *El Tigre* opted to raft up alongside *Eagle,* let off her twenty wet and wild-eyed passengers, and then go out to her storm mooring in the bay. You see, the docks became rough and sometimes untenable during a southerly wind and all the boats berthed there had storm mooring out in the safety of the bay. Luck was in it for most of the boats that remained at the dock that day. The proprietor, Michele, had just finished building a breakwater the day before that gave ample protection for the boats in the marina.

Let me tell you something, it started to blow! That green squall was no squall but the start of a two-day storm that we would much later find out was named Klaus. We clocked seventy-eight knots of wind in the gusts as I borrowed a Boston Whaler to go out and grab the crew off of *El Tigre*. With a building swell I had to run up alongside the sixty-foot cat and get the crew off, one at a time. I secured a twenty-foot painter to a cleat on the deck of the cat then motored quickly alongside as one crew would jump into the Whaler and then we would be pushed backwards to the end of the line by the passing swell. Then I would go again. That was when the fishing boat *Mahalo* dragged by and onto the new breakwater protecting the marina. "Mahalo" means thank you in Hawaiian and I was thankful that there was no one on board that doomed craft.

It blew all night, and by morning there were two boats washed up on the beach. The waves had pounded them to nothing. It was as if they melted into the sand. The sand bar in the middle of the bay had breaking waves at about five feet. Two of the Windjammer Barefoot Cruise ships were in the harbor with guests aboard. The *Polynesia* put to sea, while the *Yankee Clipper* decided to ride the weather out on anchor. No one really expected this thing to last long, although the *Poly* returned after the storm had abated with one guest sporting a broken leg. The *Yankee Clipper?* I'll tell you more on that later, but some of the yachts in the marinas went out on anchor while others braved the breaking bar and got out of the bay altogether.

A visiting Swan 65 got out, leaving one of its crew stranded in the restaurant at the marina. I took her under my wing and we helped boats in the marina double lines and found extra fenders for *Eagle,* which was now stuck on the end of the fuel dock and slamming it with authority. By nightfall it was still howling and boats were going onto the beach left and right. A ferry boat that had lost one prop on a tangled anchor fought the swell the entire day trying to pull boats off of the beach, across the bar, and out of the bay. She finally succumbed to the storm herself and ended up in the jumble ashore.

Nightfall and it was still storming out. I took my newfound friend over to the French side of the island and Marigot to see if her Swan 65 had ended up over there. They were not to be found so I treated her to dinner at David's Restaurant. It was there that I watched a sealed waterproof VHF bag expand like a balloon in about five minutes. The owner remarked, "Wow! There must be a low pressure system around here somewhere." That was when we finally got the picture, and Klaus ended up being his name!

We beat feet back to Phillipsburg just in time to see the *Yankee Clipper* drag anchors onto the bar, go over on her side, and jettison eighty guests into the bay. So we spent the night saving lives. By first light there were only three boats left riding out the storm. It was still gusting to eighty knots and the beach was chock-a-block with wrecked boats. The air was full of spume, seaweed, and the smell of diesel fuel. It made our eyes smart and we were crying from the scene of devastation.

One of the three boats, *El Tigre,* was about to give up the ghost. There was so much water in the air that her engine would not run. The owner, Malcolm, and the skipper, David, decided to try and sail her out. First they had to swim out and climb on board. Then they realized that they could not put her dagger boards down as she had to sail over the bar. The cat drew too much water with the boards down. With just a storm jib up they vainly tried to claw off of the lee shore, but without dagger boards the helm became too much and the steering cables parted. Here you had the skip sitting on one of the aft hulls steering the tiller by hand while the owner tacked and set the storm jib again and again but making no headway. We on the beach were in finger-crossed anticipation, cursing or praying at every inch lost that somehow, some way, they could save the boat. But in the end the feat proved impossible, so David picked a spot between two wrecked yachts and sailed her onto the beach at about twenty knots. *El Tigre* took the bowsprit off a cruising boat and the rig out of a Swan 39 as she flew up high and dry. It was quite a sight, to say the least!

Only two boats were left, and one finally dragged her anchors but miraculously hooked up on a sunken boat just outside the shore break and survived. Another sixty-foot cat named *Maho* managed to keep her engine running and motored for twenty-four hours against the swell and wind while still on her storm mooring. We took turns swimming jerry cans of fuel out to the owner who manned the helm non-stop, never giving up the fight. The sea was too rough to climb on board so you had to sit in the water while the owner left the helm, boat-hooked the jerry cans away from you, and then you had to swim back to shore through all the seaweed and fuel...not nice. The poor little quarter-tonner *Kitchema* ended up holed on the beach without a rig, and its owner's fifty-eight-foot cruising ketch, which was in her slip behind the breakwater, had ripped her windless out of the deck and finished the storm sitting on the dock. And that brand new breakwater, well, it didn't exist anymore!

But what became of Klaus, our unnamed storm? They finally got around to that...the next day! Oh, archives had it tracked as a tropical storm, but they forgot to tell the weathermen living in the Antilles. It was a minimal hurricane at eighty knots of wind as it passed between Puerto Rico and the U.S. Virgin Islands and continued out to harass shipping for another three days. However, eighty knots and a lee shore make for impossible conditions in the yachting world, and two days of it was insult added to injury. But we learned not to depend on the local weatherman during hurricane season, and the day after Klaus there was a run on weather faxes at the local marine store.

Chapter 8

What You Don't Know Won't Hurt You

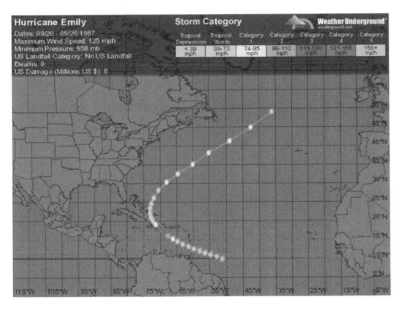

September 26, 1987
"Emily"

Ocean racing...what a way to make a living! The Newport to Bermuda Multihull Race, The Carlsberg 500, The Bermuda One/Two, The Around Long Island Race, The Newport to Boston Race; all were part of the 1987 New England Multihull Circuit, and I was once again sponsored. This time it was with a great little class IV catamaran named *Skyjack* that was a forty-five-foot ocean-racing machine built in the island nation of St. Kitts in the West Indies. I had completely refitted her the winter of 1986 and with enough—but not a lot of—money commenced to campaign her. Off I went, flying the colors of St. Kitts, ocean racing in America. What a season.

This was still in the days of sextant navigation, VHF radio communication with a range limited to line of sight, and Loran C that only worked near shore and never in Bermuda. Single-sideband transmitters were available but heavy, took tremendous battery power to operate, and were very expensive. Suffice to say I did not have one. Shoots, I didn't even have wind instruments or an in-the-hull speedometer at the time, which in hindsight was probably a good thing.

It was pretty much seat of your pants sailing and we did well. Finishing in the top three every race as well as breaking the Newport to Bermuda record built confidence in myself as well as in *Skyjack*. By season's end I was ready for anything. Because September and the cold came along up in New England it was time to head back to the islands of the Caribbean for the winter racing season. Putting together a crew of four was easy with the reputation the boat had made for herself, and I recruited two inshore multihull sailors who had never been offshore in an ocean cat before, as well as my International One Design skipper, Boots. With two on a watch and four hours on four hours off, the seven hundred-plus miles to Bermuda and the eight hundred-plus miles to St. Kitts would be a breeze, if you will pardon the expression.

Before departure I had checked the weather, of course, and noted that a tropical storm, Emily, which had crossed St. Vincent in the Windward Islands and had strengthened to a hurricane with 110 knots of wind when it beat up on the Dominican Republic, had left that island as a minimal gale and was forecast to diminish over the Bahamas. I opted to shove off and wait in Bermuda to see if anything else developed before pushing on to the Caribbean.

Sailing *Skyjack* with an experienced crew was a dream. We would set the autopilot and deploy the trailing log...yes, we had the old trailing Walker Log that would be dragged like a small torpedo behind the boat letting us know our relative speed. This worked up to fourteen knots, at which time it would start jumping out of the water, doing nothing but attracting large fish that would then try to eat it. We carried extras. I also made a rule...below ten knots of boat speed we would shake the reef in the sails; above fourteen knots we would put them back in. If we got down to very little sail, we would let the boat go just as fast as it wanted to go and hang on. After all, she was a GREAT boat.

We got down to very little sail. Nothing but a reefed staysail, wind, waves and water...lots of water. We let the old girl have her reins and off she went slamming like John Henry to beat the steam pile driver. It was loud, it was rough, and the crew was worried. But I knew *Skyjack* could take it and told them so. We just held on, hunkered down in our foul weather gear, and let the autopilot drive. I don't know how hard the wind blew as we had no instruments or how high the waves got as it was night, but thirty feet seemed small at the moment. On a close reach and flying with water everywhere made me think of my first bad weather at sea, Hurricane Frederick in 1979, but we were running in that storm. This time it was a slam, a very fast slam, until morning, and after only seventy hours we arrived at Bermuda.

Strange??? There was no Bermuda Harbor Radio on the air. Normally you called them as you approached and they vectored you into St. George's Cut by radar, much like an air traffic controller, but at sea. There was no sea buoy at St. David's Light; there were no channel markers in St. George's Cut! It was blowing thirty to forty knots, water in the air and white caps galore. *Skyjack's* motor didn't want to start, so we sailed into St. George's to find…a mess!

There were boat wrecks everywhere, capsized catamarans, and cruising yachts high and dry on the little rock islands that dotted the harbor. There wasn't a tree standing and hardly a roof visible. RAF helicopters were flying about and there was an air of concern, to say the least. Upon mooring alongside the customs dock, or rather what was left of it, and inquiring what had happened, we were informed that there had been a hurricane that morning! "Well, no wonder the weather was so bad!" is what I told the crew. They were awestruck. Boots was so impressed with *Skyjack* that upon the eventual arrival in the West Indies she went on to purchase and sail the boat with B.J., another renowned American woman sailor, in the Two-star... the two-handed transatlantic race from Plymouth, England, to Newport, Rhode Island.

Emily, did someone say Emily? The last we had heard of her she was to dissipate over the Bahamas. What had transpired? Well, that little girl had made history. Not only was she the strongest hurricane to hit Bermuda in thirty-nine years, she had done it running at forty knots! Most storms travel between five and twenty-five knots, the slower being the meaner. This little compact mighty mite had zoomed across the Atlantic slamming Bermuda with hurricane force winds for ten minutes and went out to sea, increasing to fifty knots of forward motion. Winds were to 110 knots for that devastating ten minutes and the damage was evident. Ninety percent of all the trees were down. Two hundred homes lost their roofs, and in Bermuda roofs are made of lime rock! One cruise ship in the harbor at Hamilton had ripped out the bollards holding her to the dock and had gone adrift. One fellow towing an Etchells (a small one design sailboat) with a seventeen-foot Boston Whaler lost the sailboat as it sank then had the Whaler blow over. He, now in the water, was blown out toward the sea. But as the eye of the storm passed so quickly, he was then blown back to shore.

And the classic tourist story: The man said he had never been in a hurricane before so he ventured out to experience it. "I should have known better when the sign blew by and hit me in the head" was his quote in the local newspaper. He, however, carried on, tried to rescue a small boat that was breaking loose, and jumped on board just as it did exactly that—broke loose and headed out to sea and sank! He had his wits enough to grab a life jacket and luck enough to have been noticed by the crew of a cruise ship anchored out in the bay. As he blew by in the fury, they put a lifeboat over and went out to save his silly ass. Talk about luck. That guy must have said his prayers when he woke up in the morning rather than at night before he went to sleep is all I have to say.

After the calm set in and the British military arrived to save the day, we also heard other peculiar stories. One: that about ten thousand bobolinks, yes, bobolinks, a migratory bird that travels in the fall from Canada to South America, had been caught up in the storm. They must have been around the Bahamas when Emily took them on the ride of their lives and deposited them on Bermuda where they remain to this day. As did thousands of Connecticut warblers, and where they came from is anybody's guess. And then there was the story of the sailboat that entered the harbor and flew up and down the bay in St. George's at about twenty knots, sailing back and forth, back and forth, looking for a place to tie up as if it was a Sunday picnic sail. Didn't they realize that a hurricane had just passed? That would be us.

Chapter 9

Now You See Me...Now You Don't

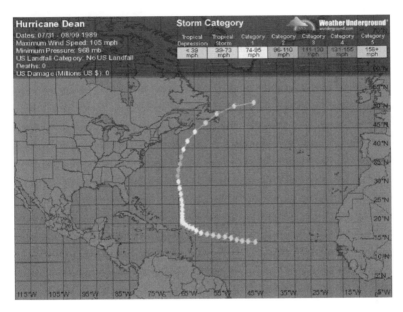

Hurricane Dean
Dates: 07/31 - 08/09 1989
Maximum Wind Speed: 105 mph
Minimum Pressure: 968 mb
US Landfall Category: No US Landfall
Deaths: 0
US Damage (Millions US $): 0

Storm Category — Weather Underground

Tropical Depression	Tropical Storm	Category 1	Category 2	Category 3	Category 4	Category 5
< 38 mph	39-73 mph	74-95 mph	96-110 mph	111-120 mph	121-155 mph	156+ mph

August 2–3, 1989
"Dean"

One thing that is predictable about hurricanes is that they are unpredictable. Now that is a fact. As the height of the hurricane season approached with the beginning of August, Dean formed between the Cape Verde Islands and the West Indies. Hurricanes formed out in that part of the Eastern Atlantic are called Cape Verde storms and have the highest potential to become devastating tempests. Dean, a small and compact mighty mouse, bee-lined it for where I had my current charge, *Sir Walter Wally*, a Standfast 40 sloop—that would be a sailboat with one mast—hauled out for safe keeping and also where I was once again skippering the maxi cat *Eagle*. Thus while making bacon by day sailing the cat from St. Maarten to St. Barth with up to twenty-five guests on board, the crew and I were called on to evacuate that little French island of any tourist who missed the last plane out. After all, it was the day that the storm was predicted to hit.

There were thirty-two people on the dock when we arrived about eleven a.m., bags and all. We didn't waste any time as the storm was for certain threatening and we had to get back to St. Maarten, get these people off the boat, grab all of our storm gear, and make the five o'clock p.m. Simpson Bay Bridge, called "the Five O'clock Bridge," into the safety of the Dutch side of the island's lagoon. After the "Five O'clock Bridge" there would be no other opening until after the storm had passed.

Ah, lovely St. Barth; we zoomed in and zoomed out...well, almost. On the way out we passed the anchored 232-foot motor yacht *Non Stop*, the same mega yacht I had received a weather fax from prior to the sneak attack of Hurricane Klaus in 1984. The crew hailed us and they too asked to be evacuated. It seemed that the owner of the yacht, Mr. Kings had run out of money and had not enough fuel on board to move anywhere. He just traded away on board on his commodities schemes using up what little fuel that was left to run the generators and keep the air conditioners running and the computers happy, hoping for a windfall…no pun intended…but did anyone catch the irony of the name of that boat? I wondered.

As the storm neared, the wind shifted north as usual and we had a close beat back to St. Maarten, arriving around two thirty in the afternoon. A close beat back, which is having the wind just off to the side of the nose, to St. Maarten is a rarity as normally the wind is behind you making it a run back. A beat back in August usually means there is a storm a-coming, and it will be arriving soon! As soon as all the evacuees were off, we grabbed all our ground tackle used for a storm—extra food and water, flashlights and batteries, foul weather gear, the works—and headed along the coast to Simpson Bay and to the entrance of the lagoon. What a mess that was! With thirty boats jonesing to get in, all milling about in complete disarray, this was panic time and an accident waiting to happen.

Thus as the bridge opened, it was the French who made the mad dash for the entrance. *Quicksilver*, a sixty-foot motor catamaran, crashed two more of his compatriots and almost blocked the bridge opening for the rest of us, which would have been a catastrophe. Luckily for us, they all were French, which meant that they could easily extricate themselves from any unwanted situations with aplomb. All yelling quelled and aside, the three yacht captains figured out in which order *they* would enter the lagoon and allowed the rest of us to follow. I prudently waited until the next to last boat passed and then I entered. You see, taking a half-a-million-dollar cat that is thirty feet wide through a bridge entrance that is thirty-four feet wide will put grey hair on one's head!

I decided to put the boat at the end of the lagoon, down near the airport and the Turtle Pier Bar. There were not very many anchored boats at that end, and anchored boats could be a problem if they got loose during the passing maelstrom. Also, as the wind shifted after the eye of the storm had passed, *Eagle* would find herself at the top of the lagoon and out of the anchor-dragging line of fire of any boats that would have tripped their anchors upon the 180-degree wind shift. Novices wondered at my strategy; the vets informed them that I had done this drill before.

We set three anchors in a wide array to cover any wind shift from the beam forward and also to allow for the swing and reset as the wind turned. Another large storm anchor was prepared but left on deck in case of the unlikely chance that all three anchors dragged or the likely scenario of a loose cannon-type anchor-dragging boat ensnaring our set anchors, which would then have to be cut away.

Eagle being secure, the crew and I decided to head over to a friend's Turtle Pier Bar, which was right on the lagoon with a dock, restaurant/bar, and, yes, turtles. Every captain and every crew were there awaiting the coming of Dean. That would mean a proper piss-up, a true West Indian Hurricane Party, was about to ensue. We dove right in. David, the captain of the famous catamaran *El Tigre* of hurricanes past, took up the laurels of emcee and commenced with stand-up comedy accompanied by drinking games and an impromptu round of Trivial Pursuit. As the night wore on, he and I would run across the street to the Met Office in the airport, which is the Dutch weather center for the island, to get the hourly update on the storm's position and return to a hushed crowd and distribute the news. Yes, the thing was coming. Yes, it was small: seventy-eight to one hundred knots of wind, and landfall was inevitable, well, eighty percent inevitable. And the party would commence again.

Midnight came and August third began with David and me once more running across to the Met Office. Traffic was nil by now. The wind was still north of east at about thirty knots; the same direction but a little stronger than the wind we had beat back into from St. Barth and the sky was oddly clear. The difference this time was that the Met Office had this little bastard on radar! Dean was sixty miles out and the center pressure had dropped to 20.5 inches. Hell! The barometer on most boats only registers to twenty-two inches! Once David and I returned to the hushed crowd and informed them that the edge of the storm was only sixty miles out and that the bottom had fallen out of the barometer, a full-on stampede was started as everyone headed for their boats. Tenders and dinghies were lifted aboard and lashed down. VHF radios all tuned to a common communication channel and everyone hunkered down waiting for the first onslaught of the telltale gusts.

And it missed!!! Good ole Dean just hung a right and just like that...zoom, it was gone. Well, gone to Bermuda, but gone from us. The wind continued to blow thirty knots or so out of the northeast, then later in the morning shifted to the south for a day. And that was it. So, as we say in the West Indies, "Jah move in strange ways." You got to thank Him for that!

Chapter 10

In the Beverly Hills of Hurricane Holes

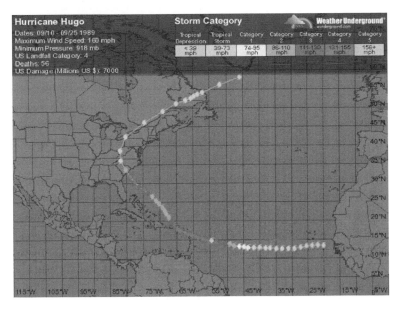

September 17–18, 1989
"Hugo"

By mid-September, a few more storms had developed, like Erin that had missed by a long shot but still called for the evacuation of the leftover tourists in St. Barth. Not much came of it except that the crew on the mega yacht *Non Stop* once again asked to be included with the *Eagle* evacuees, and once again the owner opted to stay, saying that he would "go down with the ship." Well, the storm didn't even touch the island but he, ole Mr. Kings, gave it up anyway. Failing at his commodities trading, he decided to pull the plug on the boat, draw a hot bath, and rest soothingly in the tub with a bottle of gin until the ship went down.

He was found there about a month later by Wilson McQueen, the pioneer of scuba diving in the Caribbean and founder of diving in the Dutch island of Saba as well as the company Saba Deep. We were assisted by a couple of gendarmes while diving in search of a corpse so as to settle the insurance claims by the family. Interpol had searched the world, finding nothing. Wilson had a feeling "Kings" was still down there and went to prove it. A few weeks later Hurricane Gabrielle missed the island but became a category 5 storm completely destroying the resort area of Cancun and sending us giant surf to play in.

However, a few days after that miss, Hugo formed in the Atlantic and started his long, sweeping curve of destruction through the Lesser Antilles, the U.S. Virgin Islands, and Puerto Rico. He ended his trounce smashing into Charleston, South Carolina, causing what was up until then the most costly storm in U.S. history.

For this storm, the West Indies were completely prepared so there was no call for *Eagle* to evacuate those foolish leftovers who thought to weather the storm in St. Barth. Through prudence, divine guidance, or simply from coming to their senses, the tourists had all gone home, a bummer for those who happened to live in Charleston! The hurricane hunter planes from Puerto Rico had been flying into the storm every two hours since the thirteenth of September and found a category 4 storm, winds to 165 knots (which is a lot, 189.75mph) and a central pressure of 918mb. Hugo was setting up to be a dangerous and deadly storm, not to be taken lightly!

Raking French Guadeloupe with destruction on the seventeenth and on across the other West Indian islands of Montserrat, Nevis, St. Kitts, Statia, and on to St. Croix in the USVI, the center of the storm luckily passed twenty-eight miles from us in St. Maarten, but its wrath was evident. I had placed *Eagle* in the same spot as I had for Hurricane Dean and with the veteran crew on board. *Sir Walter Wally,* my little Standfast 40 sloop, was back in the water and my home so I manned her. I placed her in the newly built marina in Anse Marcel on the French side of the island.

In 1987, I had been the first boat to reside in Anse Marcel and through the use of my big mouth had encouraged others to keep their yachts there too. As a reward, the captain of the port always kept a berth open for me in times of inclement weather. The marina is a tight little spot excavated out of an old salt pond with a meandering entrance opening up into a basin surrounded on three sides by tall hills and on the fourth by a four-star hotel. Mooring is alongside floating docks anchored to huge boulders by steel cables. It is all safe, safe, and very...safe.

I was by myself as I pulled *Sir Walter* alongside Mad Dog's *Details,* a Newport 41. He and his mate and killer girlfriend Celia helped me spider-web my boat into the confines of the marina. I had known Mad Dog since the early '70s and stories of surf in Hawaii, catamaran sailing in Maui, and the voyaging of the great schooner *Teragram,* and no, "Mad Dog" is not his real name. Celia is a gorgeous fireball of a Brazilian and a famous ocean racer in her own right.

I was then in my jeep and off to the airport. You see, to my friend Claudia, one of the original Americans on the island and who had been visiting there since the '60s as a child, I had promised that I would meet her friend Michelle and sail her over to St. Barth. Michelle hated the radical landing at the airport in St. Barth, and besides that, the airport was closed because of the approaching storm. On a normal day, sailing to St. Barth would have posed no problem, but with Hugo knocking at the door, sailing over and getting back safely was out of the question.

Now Michelle, who I had met in passing only once, was, on a scale of beauty from one to ten, an eleven. And of course being an international traveler she had heard every pick-up line in the book. So when I informed her that she would not to be sailing over to St. Barth but would have to stay with me for the night due to an approaching storm...well, of course she did not believe me. That is, until she saw all the yachts spider-webbed into the marina at Anse Marcel. And she made the best of it, and that was to me the beginning of a wonderful relationship lasting six years, until

Hurricane Luis loomed...but that is another chapter in the book, so read on!

Even with the eye of the storm passing alongside the neighboring Dutch island of Statia, it still blew stink in St. Maarten, 125 knots by us. But that did not stop us from raging. It was, after all, a grand reason for a hurricane party. Mad Dog, Celia, Michelle, and I were with all the other captains and crews at Le Privelege, the nightclub up the hill until the power went out. That was when I loaded us, the club manager, and ten other yachties into and onto my jeep, and down the hill we went to the marina and hotel. At the gate the Haitian guards tried to stop us and make me park my jeep in the lot under the trees. But all fifteen of us were having none of that. Besides, I just knew those trees were not going to be there in the morning, at least not standing, and woe be to any car parked underneath. It was off and through the gate and INTO the hotel with my jeep we went. And you know, in the end, I was right about those trees.

As the storm raged, the party continued. It was odd because I had radio contact with the crew on *Eagle* and it seemed that the lagoon was in a shit fight. Boats were breaking loose left and right, mostly because the St. Kitts Coast Guard cutter was loose and driving around in the storm in a panic chopping up with its props the anchor roads of storm-moored yachts. These in sequence would either foul another moored yacht or drag through the lagoon passing the anchored *Eagle* and off into the white, barely missing the long black catamaran. The crew claimed that I had left them at the end of the bowling alley!

When the crew asked how we were faring, Mad Dog claimed that we were in the "Beverley Hills of

Hurricane Holes." With the champagne flowing and the exorbitant price we were paying for dockage, it was not far from the truth. But as I listened to the turmoil my crew was going through I realized that the expense of Anse Marcel was marginal compared to the cost of a paint job that would ensue if a loose yacht dragged down the side of my boat.

As the night wore on and into the black of the morning we did witness some gnarly knockdowns of a couple of yachts across the way due to passing williwaws funneling down the hills. One floating dock twisted itself free and capsized, revealing a plethora of barnacles that wanted to abrade the hull of the new Frers 51 *Margaux*. She was, in my opinion, the first beautiful boat that Beneteau had built and had been built from the mold of the Swedes' International 50 race boat *Carat*. She was worth saving. We came to her aid by slinging some spare tires between the two, protecting both boat and barnacle, and saved the day. You got the picture: the four of us trotted around being damage control central. Making sure everyone was safe and secure, we wandered the docks sipping champagne and thoroughly enjoying the adventure.

We decided to wander over to the beach to see what the ocean was up to, but flying shingles from the pool area put a stop to that idea. Entering the hotel we found panic among the tourists and led them to calm by pretending to communicate via the VHF to the authorities that be and rendering a sense of comfort to the unnerved. The hotel management did its best also, keeping the kitchen open and serving hot food throughout the night due to the advantage of having an in-house generator. That helped to keep the guests below the level of hysteria.

About four in the morning (the shit hits the fan *always* at four in the morning), we ran out of champagne. Both stores in *Sir Walter Wally* and *Details* had been depleted. The owner of *Margaux* had come down and donated his cave to us for saving his yacht and we still ran out. It was Mad Dog's idea to go up and roust the nightclub manager from her hotel room and visit the nightclub. Lending her foul weather gear and her being such a sport, it was into the jeep, out of the hotel, and up the hill we went...just in time to catch two thieves breaking into the storeroom of the club! The Dog and I ran them off sans their truck which we decommissioned for them and, voila, the manager gave us a case of Crystal champagne as a reward.

Boarding back up the smashed storeroom door, we were once again back down the hill and partying with the crews. By six in the morning we had one of them on *Details* and, having ice cubes and a sewing needle, we pierced his ear using a champagne cork as a backing, and Mad Dog gave him his emerald earring to fill the void. We finished off the last of the pâté, brie, and walnuts and began to wonder when exactly the storm would abate. Michelle and I went back to my boat to take a nap, the sailor with the pierced ear decide to drive home to his wife, and Hugo decided to go and beat up on St. Croix.

By nine a.m. the storm was over. Celia came by our boat with aspirin on a pillow and two bloody Marys saying that we would need this age-old Brazilian remedy. Mad Dog and I jumped in the jeep and went for a tour of the island passing the now tree-filled parking lot with cars underneath. Farther along we ran across the ear-pierced fellow stuck in a ditch and wondering what story he was going to tell his wife...I mean, being out all night, hung over, emerald earring, wearing a bloody shirt and all. After helping him on his way by dragging his vehicle out of the ditch with the jeep, we continued over to the lagoon and Simpson Bay.

What a mess. *Eagle* was fine, but the pile of yachts behind her and ashore was sickening. There were boats in the road, cars in the lagoon, and Jim's A-frame home had washed into the sea. Perhaps you remember this famous photographer, for he was the photo-nut who was busted during the 1983 America's Cup trying to take a photo of the hidden keel of the winning twelve-meter sailboat, *Australia II.* Anyway, after the storm had passed, he had taken a photo from the open front door of his living room and bar area all awash by waves...his "wet bar" he called it. Roofs were missing everywhere and the ocean was full of big waves and debris. It was a little sobering after our night in Beverly Hills. I took it as a lesson luckily earned. And I also noted that the storms seemed to be getting a little stronger every year.

*A car in the parking lot; this is what
a hurricane will do.*

Chapter 11

Out of the Frying Pan and Into the Fire

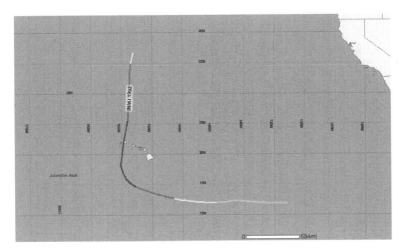

September 12, 1992
"Iniki"

By the end of the 1989 hurricane season, I was getting a little tired of weathering storms in the Caribbean. Luckily for me, I was asked to help project manage a new type of sailboat that was to be built in Florida. Sending off *Sir Walter Wally* with a friend to Bequia, I packed up and headed for the west coast of Florida and the old Morgan Yard near Tampa to commence the building of *Amoco Procyon*, a custom sixty-five-foot showboat.

The Procyon Project was the brainchild of Olaf Harken of Harken Yacht Equipment, and he, along with sixty-five sponsors, decided to build a show platform for the cutting-edge technology of American yacht building to date. The boat was to have a canting keel, water ballast, push-button hydraulic controls, state-of-the-art computer/satellite navigation, handicap access, a carbon fiber bipod mast and free-standing carbon boom, just to mention a few of the innovations. I was to be the skipper.

Spending a year in the Tampa area building the boat and then two years non-stop sailing, racing, and showing kept me out of the hurricane belt. None seemed to follow me to Florida's Gold Coast. Hurricane Bob in 1991 blasted Newport, Rhode Island, as we were sailing out of the Great Lakes, and all we had to do was punch across Lake Erie in the worst weather I had ever seen at sea, worse than Emily in 1987...And we were in a lake!

Touring the Midwest, Canada, New England, the East Coast, and even a ten-week jaunt to the West Indies for regattas and never seeing a storm lulled me into a sense of comfort. By 1992, and about eighteen thousand miles under *Procyon's* keel, it was time for a refit in Newport before the show went on. The boat was to be in a shed for two or three months and I opted for a well-needed vacation.

Using my birthday as an excuse and a friend with a plane as the mode of transportation, I decided to head out to the Bahamas for a month to my old haunt on the island of Eleuthera. I had been surfing there since the '60s, and friends and I had built an A-frame there in the early '70s as a rustic home away from home, and it was always available for shelter during a surfari. Preparing for the trip I noticed a storm threatening the area and we held off for a day.

Andrew, a category 5 storm, rumbled through producing a ten-mile-wide scar of devastation across the Bahamas and Florida. We took the plane over Eleuthera to see the aftermath and it was unbelievable! The village of Lower Bouge had disappeared under the onslaught of a tidal wave created after the storm had passed, and Upper Bouge was a mass of matchsticks. And farther on up the island by Surfer's Beach, the little A-frame...well, to this day, when I meet a beautiful woman I will in jest offer her my house in the Bahamas...if she can find it. There was not even debris! Usually the toilet remains, but after Andrew got through with the island only the underground cistern remained intact.

I returned to Newport and the boatyard in a bit of a gloom. But the very next day, my old friend Captain Andy from Kauai and Hurricane Iwa fame contacted me. Not knowing anything about my Hurricane Andrew trauma, Andy simply said he kind of missed me and the good ole days and wondered if I would like to come out to Hawaii on a sort of working vacation. It would seem that he needed a skipper to sail his forty-two-foot cat on the weekends up the Na Pali Coast. I could work three days a week and surf four days out on the island of Niihau if I wanted.

Yes, Niihau, the Forbidden Island. One of Hawaii's eight islands, Niihau is nearest to Kauai and is off limits to almost everyone. In 1864 the island was purchased from Queen Liliuokalani of the kingdom of Hawaii by Elizabeth Sinclair, later Robinson, a wealthy New Zealand rancher, for $10,000 worth of gold. Aubrey Robinson, Elizabeth's grandson, closed the island in 1915 to anyone not of Hawaiian blood. His idea was to preserve the Hawaiian bloodline that existed almost entirely on the island and that was quickly disappearing from all the other islands since the overthrow of the kingdom in 1898 by the United States. Somehow Captain Andy had befriended the current owners and controllers of the island, Bruce and Keith, who allowed Andy to surf there as long as he did not come ashore. What an honor, I thought.

Talk about going from gloom to bloom! I would not have missed that chance for the world! I immediately called Michelle who was at moment working in California and asked her if she would go out to Hawaii with me. She said yes and I flew into L.A. for a rendezvous. We spent two days visiting friends on the Cal coast and enjoying the sights. I rarely make it out to California. The interval also blunted the jet lag as well as let me catch up on what the weather in the Pacific was up to.

Weather wise, I was more concerned with the size and direction of Pacific swells for surfing rather than approaching storms. Hawaii was not known for hurricanes, so when I watched the news the evening before Michelle and I departed for the islands I was surprised to see in the satellite photo what looked like a hurricane threatening the state. It wasn't even mentioned by the weatherman in his nightly report, but my curiosity had been aroused. I immediately called American Airlines and asked about the status of the flight...was it to be cancelled, delayed? Why, they did not know anything about it. It was business as usual.

Arriving at the terminal in the morning we found it packed with tourists like us headed out to the fun and sun. The plane was full, full, full. Checking in, I asked again about the threat of a hurricane and received a chuckle and assurance from the guy at the counter. He told me that Hawaii *never* gets hurricanes. Had he never heard of Iwa is what I thought. Sitting at the gate I patiently waited for the call for boarding when the captain and first officer passed close to me. The captain was saying, "...and when we get to Honolulu, we are going to get these people off the plane and then get that plane the fuck out of there!" *Rut Row* is what I was thinking. We boarded anyway and flew into Oahu with a bird's eye view of the entire fleet in Pearl Harbor heading out to sea! Déjà vu and memories of the Hawaiian hurricane of 1982 ran through my head.

And the airport was closed. Hundreds of people were stranded; there were no flights out, no busses in, and no taxis. It seemed there was a hurricane warning and that within twenty-four hours we would be experiencing hurricane force winds, high seas, and danger of bodily harm. The Boy Scout in me took over and I flagged down an empty bus, the driver heading for home. Speaking the pidgin I had learned during my visit in '82, I convinced the driver to go back and get one more load of tourists before he called it quits. It was just the right thing to do, him being local and all and we tourists being at the mercy of the island, the *aina* in Hawaii, the spirit of the land or the aloha spirit, and under the influence of Tutu Pele the pagan Hawaiian goddess whose daughter Leahi lived in the Diamond Head crater. I mean, was he "Pau already?" a pidgin term for finished or done. I must have impressed him with that gibberish, for around he went for one last load.

Well, we maxed out that bus and I gave those tourists a speech that brightened the Hawaiian driver's eyes. I told them about the man and how he should not even be here. I told them that it was the stupid airline authorities' fault that had put us in harm's way. I explained how our driver should be home boarding up his house, protecting his wife and children, stocking up on extra water, food, and the likes because it could get very bad, very soon. And then I explained about *aina,* the land and the aloha spirit that only the true Hawaiians still seemed to hold dear on the islands. That, I reasoned, was why he had come back for us. He was not on the clock; he was not under the employ of the people who had brought us here. And then I pulled out a $20 bill, handed it to the lad, and while jumping off the bus, I reminded all of them: always remember to tip while in the islands!

I must give the weathermen credit, they are forecasters to be sure, and on the ninth, Iniki was 470 nautical miles southeast of Hilo, Hawaii, on the Big Island and no threat to land. She had amazingly started as a tropical wave off the coast of Africa and sauntered across the Atlantic Ocean. Bouncing off the mountains of Central America, she had somehow survived to exit into the Pacific and become tropical storm Iniki. Cruising westward through the Pacific, she strengthened to a mere eighty-five-knot storm, but by the eleventh of September she was causing stress at Pearl and Honolulu International, not to mention Kauai, where she was bound to make landfall in the next twenty-four to forty-eight hours. Being 130 nautical miles southwest of Lihue, Kauai, and packing winds to 125 knots and having a 938mb central pressure, she was heading on a dangerous track for what looked like a mirror image of Iwa ten years before.

I took Michelle under tow and headed back into the airport seeing if we could find some flight over to Kauai. As luck (whether bad or good) would have it, there was one plane going over empty. Their job was to evacuate the filming crew of the movie *Jurassic Park*, who had been left stranded. Shades of *Eagle* and the evacuations of St. Barth is what I was thinking. I convinced them that we were hurricane consultants and that they would need us desperately over there, and onto the plane we went.

Landing on Kauai, we found the island in a bit of a panic to be sure. With no public transportation here either we simply stuck our thumbs out and grabbed a ride that took us eventually to Captain Andy's. To this day I cannot remember where exactly his house was because the face of the island was to change so drastically. Suffice to say that we arrived in time to tell him that tape would do no good on the windows. I filled him in on the fact that the shingles on the house next door would be coming right through those taped windows, so we broke out the three-quarter-inch plywood. Boarding everything up, we turned to filling the tubs and Jacuzzi with fresh water, breaking out the candles and lighters, and stocking the fridge. I had called Andy from California and told him that IF a storm did threaten he shouldn't install the new generator into his forty-two-foot cat as yet. He may need it after his boat was wrecked. All in jest, of course, but boy, how close to the center of the nail can one hit!

On the twelfth, the storm made landfall with the wind sustained at 145 knots gusting to 175 knots. That would be around 202 miles per hour in land-lubber terms. I wondered how duct tape would fare when the wind breeched 200 miles per hour. Iniki was a noisy one. The corner of the house kept lifting off but the roof, after letting the rain blow in, would then snap shut. It seemed safe enough in the house until those aforementioned shingles started to fly. They came through the three-quarter-inch ply. They came through the solid wood doors! One bounced off my bed and stuck in the closet door, for chrissake. That was when we opted for outdoors between Andy's house and the other neighbor's house. There was about a twelve-foot space between the two. As we stood there in the lee of the wind we could look left and right and see the debris blowing down the road. Shit was flying everywhere when we heard this BANG!

It sounded like a gun going off, but we had no gun. Then a KABLAM, and down the road went the steel garage door. Andy surmised that the bang must have been the little window in the garage door giving way to the differences in air pressure between inside the house and out. How right he was, because all of a sudden we began to see the entire interior contents of the garage getting sucked out and blow on down the road. Bikes, surfboards, windsurfers, lawnmower, tools, you name it…it went. The truck stayed but BAM! the downstairs apartment door did not and out came the contents of that abode. Pictures, curtains, furniture, the works, as if a giant vacuum cleaner was at hand and the bag had blown off. Why, even the fold-up couch made it to the front lawn before the storm abated.

After the shingles stopped flying we figured it was safe to get back into the house and wait for the wind to quit. We were fine, no injuries, a little shook up from the show, but no worse for wear. We saw why the shingles had stopped flying: the house was no longer there! And that was just the start of the pictures of devastation I still have in my mind today. For example: all, and I mean all, of the power lines and telephone poles were down. We took off in Andy's truck and had to systematically pull them off the road to continue our tour down to Poi Pu Beach and the hotel area. Andy wanted to check on his office that was housed in the Westin. After that we planned to continue the drive to Nawiliwili Harbor to check on his cat.

As we neared Poi Pu we saw the most beautiful blue tile everywhere. We were still five miles from the beach and Andy was going ape shit! He recognized the tile as belonging to a house on the beach! We entered the hotel area, which looked to me to be a construction site. Debris was piled everywhere, quite neat piles actually, wherever the wind had left it. Picture this: bare concrete walls, no windows, no doors, no fixtures, and no paint…the wind, by God, had taken the paint off the walls. Thirty-foot waves had washed through the structures and moved the interiors to who knows where. Into the residential section we ventured and saw one entire house "maka," which in Hawaiian means toward the mountains, by about a mile and in a cane field. Its foundation was on the beach. Next door to that foundation was what was left of the blue tile-roofed house. A toilet was on the roof! I remarked to Andy after noticing the large poured concrete picnic tables that they would have made great moorings...until he informed me that they were a mile from their allotted position.

We continued on, numb, to the ship harbor at Nawiliwili. Passing a two-story house, I saw what tornados could do in the eye of a storm. The second story was completely gone. Yet up there on what was left stood the bedroom doorframe and door with a full-length mirror, unbroken. The double bed was still made and on the nightstand remained a bud vase with a rose still in it. We were absolutely amazed.

Pulling telephone poles out of the road, we continued on to the harbor. Passing the old Nawiliwili Hotel, an ancient wooden thing, I remarked that it had remained intact...until upon further scrutiny we noticed that it had moved about eight inches off its foundation. Eight inches! That meant that all the plumbing and all the wiring was broken inside! And there she sat in all her majesty, a little crooked. Turning the corner we rounded a huge stack of Budweiser beer guarded by National Guardsmen. Funny thing, the stack was in the shape of a warehouse. Yes, the warehouse was a mass of twisted metal strewn farther down the road. The plastic-wrapped six packs of canned beer had held their own.

Then we came upon the boats. They were destroyed almost entirely. A forty-five-foot Rudy Choy catamaran had literally flown through the air, colliding with the aluminum bridge deck of a 240-foot

Coast Guard cutter, destroying both that cat and the bridge deck of the cutter. One line of moored boats was on the docks while the line of boats behind them was sunk. One large sailboat was floating, one. And what of Andy's cat? Luckily he had never installed the generator.

He had moored that girl by the stern with two giant anchors down and attached them to his little cat with two two-and-three-quarter-inch hawsers. The bow he had secured to a palm tree with chain. Well, that palm tree was gone but the chain was still around the stump. The anchors were still in their same spot but those two giant lines had parted, probably like a huge elastic band, because the cat was upside down 250 feet from the water's edge, and the only mark on the ground between its resting spot on top of a one hundred-foot carbon fiber trimaran and the palm tree stump by the water was where one rudder had touched down on the cat's cartwheel to destruction. And get this, that trimaran had blown out of its shed where it was being constructed and was resting 250 feet from where that shed *used* to be! And both boats were in completely opposite directions from their points of departure. Shit like that just amazes me.

Because of the mess Iwa had caused ten years before, the state of Hawaii was prepared for Iniki. Immediately we began to see army helicopters flying in from Oahu with emergency supplies. The military set up first aid stations all over the island and dispensed medicines, ready to eat meals, and provided shelter for those of us in need. There were many who were in need: 14,380 homes were damaged, 1,421 were completely destroyed, 63 by waves alone. Funny though, if there could be humor found, I asked Andy why the old Hawaiian "plantation homes," the old, rotten, wooded structures built by the locals a hundred years ago didn't have any damage. I mean, some of these had fern growing up through the floorboards and porches. Andy's Hawaiian friends explained to me that after two thousand years of living on these islands, the locals know where the wind is *not* going to blow.

After a week of clean up, help out, and camp out, Michelle and I opted to complete our vacation on Oahu where there were things like running water and I could surf without feeling guilty about not having anyone to surf with because in Kauai we were all working to put the island back together. Oahu had its damage, mostly the Waianae side where the locals lived, but they had the same attitude as their brothers and sisters on Kauai and had cleaned up the mess. I bought a new surfboard as Andy's had all blown away and I had nothing to ride. A man came up on our last day on Kauai with a boomerang in hand that had the name of Andy's catamaran painted on it. It had been hanging over the mantle in the downstairs apartment that fateful day. The guy had found it in his garage seven miles away! All Andy could do was to ask him if he had seen any surfboards.

Upon embarking for the mainland it dawned on me how much this must affect Michelle. I mean, she had met me in 1989 during Hugo, and now here we were again, survivors of a major storm. I asked her if she thought our life a bit interesting. She thought about that one, and after rehashing my Andrew/Iniki adventure, she made some interesting observations: What was it about me that I seemed to jump from the frying pan into the fire? And did it seem that these hurricanes were following me around?

*Iniki on the Hawaiian island of Kaui.
The fury of the wind was biblical.*

Chapter 12

Never Forget to Look Over Your Shoulder

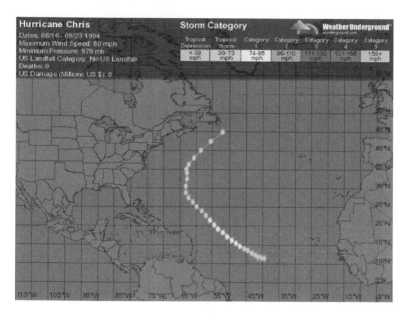

Hurricane Chris
Dates: 08/16 - 08/23 1994
Maximum Wind Speed: 80 mph
Minimum Pressure: 979 mb
US Landfall Category: No US Landfall
Deaths: 0
US Damage (Millions US $): 0

Storm Category

Tropical Depression	Tropical Storm	Category 1	Category 2	Category 3	Category 4	Category 5
< 39 mph	39-73 mph	74-95 mph	96-110 mph	111-130 mph	131-155 mph	156+ mph

August 11–September 10, 1994
"Chris"

Could it be possible that a storm would follow me around? Not a chance. Superstition, paranoia, call it what you want, it's just impossible. So Chris comes along...go figure. Now Chris wasn't a big storm and, according to the National Hurricane Center's archives, never even threatened land. It was only a hurricane for one day, on the thirteenth of August, and spent its time wandering around the Atlantic Ocean until it fell off the radar on the twenty-fourth. Just a threat to shipping...and yet found me on the tenth of September... in France!

But of course until then it was I who was at sea. With *Amoco Procyon* spending the summer marina-bound in Florida, I opted to sail off on the other Harken boat, *Nastro Azuro*, a Vallecelli sixty-five-foot ULDB doing the maxi circuit. I, my son (now that is a long story), and the skipper, Mauro, had been on the campaign since the Key West race and had finished up in Antigua Sailing Week. We were asked to deliver the yacht to Portugal for the Round Europe Race when Mauro found out that he was having a baby...well, not he but the *contessa* was having a baby with his help. So off he went to Italy, which postponed our departure until Frederico was born and August arrived. So we left late for a transatlantic crossing.

Late in the summer means no wind in the Atlantic; except of course for hurricanes, so it was a slow go across. It would seem that the developing storms off of Africa kept all the wind to themselves. Since race boats notoriously motor slowly, we were twenty-one days on the crossing with little to pique our curiosity except for Chris, a tropical storm that had developed on the eleventh and began a slow meander our way on its tour of the North Atlantic. And its moving faster than us gave us reason for concern because it seemed we were on a collision course that would meet somewhere between the West Indies and the Azores.

So we ducked south—and so did Chris. We did a feint and an uppercut, but the storm countered. A left, a right, a right, and a left and then a fake dive but with a quick turn north, and we lost her. Shoot, no wonder it took us three weeks to get across. But we made the Azores in nineteen days, put on fuel, got some wind, and absolutely flew over to Portugal in three days, too late to participate in the race but happy to be in Europe.

At Puerto Mauro, we parted company with our illustrious captain heading to Italy and the *contessa* and Frederico and we to La Rochelle and the "Grand Pavior" or boat show. I, still being sponsored by Harken, had been asked to attend the boat show and lend a hand. My son wanted to continue on, as it was his first time in Europe and visit England or anywhere they spoke English, for that matter, and go sailing. I sent him to the Admiral's Cup in Plymouth, on the English coast, the lucky dog because I hung out on the coast of France and that is where Chris found me!

Yes, Chris, the long-dead tropical storm that had passed seventy-five nautical miles from Bermuda, the closest threat to land so far. By August 25, the National Hurricane Center had declared her absorbed by a cold front pushing across the North Atlantic and that was the end of it. Well, it wasn't. Chris maintained her extra tropical characteristic as she passed south of

Greenland, Iceland, and Ireland and the British Isles. North Atlantic sailing stories told while we were in the Azores of the yachts coming from Bermuda were horrific with tales of storms, damage, and hove to delays in everyone's repertoire. A week later, curving south into the relatively warmer climate between the Azores and France, she once again put on the looks of a tropical storm, with a circular pattern and winds to seventy knots and finally made land fall at...La Rochelle and the Grand Pavior.

That's exactly where I was...exactly. We even went windsurfing the day before but the wind strength got to be too much for us. No one, it seemed, had a 3.2-meter sail! I mean, how often do the French get tropical storm force winds or tropical storms for that matter? The answer is about every hundred years! And boy did we get it. Boats blew over, the tents were in shreds. Damage was extensive, but luckily no lives were lost or boats sunk. Traffic was closed to the Ile de Re, a small island off the coast of La Rochelle, for two days due to high winds, and the boat show remained closed during that time also. Here I was, a day after my fortieth birthday having memories of my seventh birthday and Donna, and I began to wonder, I mean seriously wonder, if these things were chasing me around. Now I had to keep one eye over my shoulder. It's a creepy feeling, let me tell you. It will make you watch the weather every day from June 1 to November 30, that's for sure.

Chapter 13

My Mooring and a Bulldozer Held Me in Place

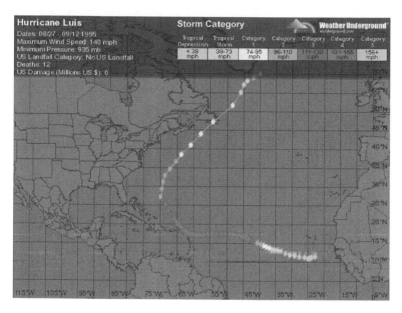

Hurricane Luis
Dates: 08/27 - 09/12 1995
Maximum Wind Speed: 140 mph
Minimum Pressure: 935 mb
US Landfall Category: No US Landfall
Deaths: 12
US Damage (Millions US $): 0

Storm Category						
Tropical Depression	Tropical Storm	Category 1	Category 2	Category 3	Category 4	Category 5
< 39 mph	39-73 mph	74-95 mph	96-110 mph	111-130 mph	131-155 mph	156+ mph

September 5, 1995
"Luis"

Ah, the good life. The Procyon Project had ended. Moving back to the West Indies, I helped to replace the catamaran that Captain Andy had lost in Hawaiian hurricane Iniki. I then delivered the fifty-eight-foot Gold Coast catamaran *Spirit of Kauai* from St. Croix in the U.S. Virgin Islands out to the Hawaiian Islands, which included a surf tour of almost all of Central America. I had skippered and sold the extraordinary sixty-eight-foot Wormwood catamaran *Indigo* to the owner of Camper and Nicholson. I was flush, had purchased the sixty-foot Spronk catamaran *Shadowfax*, and was still with Michelle. We were based out of my favorite island of St. Barth in the French West Indies doing specialized charters to the photo elite, international surfing stars, and friends. What could be better? Who knew that my dreamboat was to soon take us on a ride that would put us in magazines, a novel, on TV, featured in a documentary, and eventually as part of a movie!

As Jerry Garcia said in a Grateful Dead song: "When you think you are on easy street…there's danger at the door." Hurricane Luis had been coming across the Atlantic for a week getting big, strong, and round. However, it looked like the islands to the south, Dominica or Guadeloupe, were really going to get a hammering. A Cape Verde monster, he had started as a tropical wave on the twenty-sixth of August, became a depression the next day, and a storm by the twenty-ninth. By September third he was only six hundred nautical miles east of the Antilles with an eye having a diameter of forty miles! Peak winds were already at 146 knots (167.9 mph).

The night before, on the second, Michelle and I had a charter in St. Barth, a very romantic dinner for Faustian Ledee and his wife to celebrate their thirty-fifth wedding anniversary. They were both islanders and knew about hurricanes and were very concerned for our well-being. Finishing the charter at ten thirty the night of the second, they advised us to head south and out of harm's way. This storm was nothing to play around with. I, of course, agreed with them, and we provisioned the boat and headed out toward Antigua, Dominica, Guadeloupe, and points south.

However, with the wind being light out of the south we didn't make much headway. It was either sail at the storm or parallel to it. On top of that, the National Hurricane Center in Miami predicted a seventy-five-mile shift to the south in the next twenty-four to forty-eight hours, putting Guadeloupe in the gun sight of Luis, and after ten hours of sailing we were not even to Antigua as yet. We opted to turn around and go to my little hurricane hole on the windward side of St. Maarten.

Le Galion is inside a protective reef, a small lagoon sheltered from the north and east by a headland. From the south and west is the island itself, and the southeast quadrant is a barrier reef with a small opening, shallows that only multi-hulls can navigate, and a twenty-five-foot high wall of rocks making a point called "The Needle." Because of its difficult entrance, there were only two boats in there, Pat the proprietor's thirty-six-foot Newick trimaran, *Tryst,* and mine. Pat had put down serious storm moorings there for our boats and had weathered hurricanes in that bay since David and Frederick in 1979 without a problem. My mooring, for example, was a one hundred-pound Danforth with thirty feet of four-inch link chain going to a three-quarter-inch nylon bridle all covered with chafe gear. The anchor itself had been hand buried by Pat with a dive tank or two, leaving only the connection at the shank visible to allow frequent inspection for wear. A giant swivel was attached there to facilitate the swing. It was a serious piece of insurance, to say the least.

I honestly was not worried. We arrived two days before the storm was predicted to hit and set up camp. I took up my mooring and placed two anchors with all their rode and chain ahead and on the beach. The other two anchors I placed astern on the shallow sand bar and dug them in with the help of a dive mask, fins, and a dive tank to blow a hole in the sand. All the sails were taken off and stowed; the halyards were run up the mast to decrease windage. I even took the rudders off and placed them on the bottom alongside the mooring just in the event that if we did drag and ended up on the beach they would not be damaged. I had chafe gear out the ying yang because you never want to give chafe a chance. Even the anchor rode, fore and aft, which passed through chafing gear, were then led to cleats, and after that they were made secure to the masts. This was a very, very dangerous storm and I knew what I was doing, right…yeah right…

On Monday the fourth the wind filled in out of the north and all the yachts not in the lagoon at Simpson Bay or in hurricane survival mode somewhere else took off, and they all survived. With the wind shift also came a huge swell, effectively trapping us inside the reef whether we opted to bail or not. Running was now out of the question. So we went windsurfing. It's funny now, but I remember Pat, mimicking the Guava Berry Man, a local radio ad personality, saying, "In all me ninety-nine years on dis here island I never seen de waves come in so early before a storm hit." "Take heed," I said, and we kept on windsurfing.

That evening we got to see the storm via satellite on The Weather Channel. Wow and shit, shit, shit, were we gonna get it! And we were gonna get it BAD! Folks asked Michelle and me to stay in their houses but we refrained. I was confident with *Shadowfax,* and anyway, in the end those houses blew away too.

Back to the boat we went, got the dinghy secure in its davits, and double tied it on. Midnight or so it started to blow, forty knots on the instruments, but we were snug as a bug. Next to us *Tryst* hunkered down in the wind and sat there like a gull in a windstorm, unmoving, swaying neither left nor right yet seemed to sit down lower in the water and just hold on.

By first light the wind was gusting to one hundred, and while *Tryst* still just hunkered down, *Shadowfax* was doing a rubber band dance stretching her four anchor rodes back and forth and to the limit and then springing back. That was when one of them parted with a bang. I immediately leaped into the water with fins, mask, and snorkel and headed to shore with a replacement line in hand. After securing it to the anchor still dug in on the beach, I swam back to the boat. As a gust blew me past, I found myself swimming for my life just to stay alongside the ladder! I figured I wasn't going to do that again; let the lines part, I still had my mega mooring to fall back on.

Pat kept constant VHF radio contact with me—until his batteries went dead, at least. I got to inform him that the waves had already opened up his windsurfing shop and that the contents kept floating by us. The wind by nine a.m. was shrieking as I'd never heard before in my life. Gust to 120...130...140 were racing across the island and you heard them long before they arrived. *Shadowfax* would groan on her mooring lines and then spring ahead. *Tryst* had stopped her sit-down mode and commenced to start lifting by her nose to the limit of her triple hawsers that held her fast.

I will tell you how hard we pulled on our anchors. One of the rodes had come out of the stainless fairlead and bow roller and was chafing through the front cross-beam of the cat. As I crawled forward to return it to its proper spot by giving it a Herculean tug, it jumped back into place, thumping my forefinger so hard that I received an instant bruise on the tip and when I got back inside the deck house of the boat, I realized that the thump on my finger had blown the nail right off. Now that, my friends, is pressure! And boy did the howling increase. *Shadowfax* had custom-made sliding hatches on the deck and side of the deckhouse that we could never properly seal from the onslaught of waves while sailing so I had made vinyl covers that snapped in place over them to keep the water out. I just knew those snaps would not hold in a hurricane so I had duct taped all of them down. Believe me, I used LOTS of duct tape and that was sure working well...until about ten a.m. An exceptionally high-pitched shriek came over the mountains, and in one fell swoop all of the covers blew off—ALL! And it ain't called two hundred mile an hour tape for nothing!

With the next screaming gust I went out to see what it would do, and right beside me *Tryst* blew over... backwards! I remember sticking my head back inside and remarking to Michelle, "Boy that was a gust!" And then we started to move...And things started happening pretty damn quick.

It was gusting up to 209 mph! Why, that was just a little faster than Sprint Cup cars on the back straight of NASCAR's Daytona International Speedway! Outside the deckhouse it was white, white, and white. When I was out there I had to use a mask and snorkel to breathe and see...and I couldn't even see the bows of the boat through the spume and spray. Occasionally, in the lulls, something loomed to our right. It was a bit of grey that I thought must be the protective headland.

But for sure we were moving! We found ourselves in three-foot breaking waves. That would be what was on the sandbar behind us so I figured we must be there. I supposed that the anchors were dragging, but upon crawling forward again, I could see and feel that we hadn't pulled up on our mooring yet. So I was a little disoriented. Plan B was that if the anchors dragged I would start the 115hp outboard motor that powered *Shadowfax* (yes, the cat had an Evinrude 115 attached to a float box between the hulls, and the engine could be steered left and right from the cockpit) and I would power to relieve the strain on the mooring. I had enough gas to motor for twenty hours and it seemed time to implement Plan B.

However, there was so much water in the air the engine kept cutting out. I had had the same problem in 1987 in Hurricane Emily, and in Bermuda the same thing happening to the cat *El Tigre* in the 1984 storm Klaus. So I babied the girl to an idle and then let her warm up to dry out the insides. I noticed to my right that we were still being protected by the headland... that is, until a lull passed and I realized that the grey loom I had been seeing was not land at all but rather twenty-five-foot breaking waves on the outer reef!

That was when I saw the boat. It was a forty-five-foot catamaran surfing down the face of one of those twenty-five-foot waves. It survived the drop without pitch poling; that is, ass over teakettle, and was now heading straight for me! I gave the ole Evinrude a little gas and she died. I started her again and, in the last second, gave her full power, closed my eyes, and prayed. Off she went with one giant squirt, and the oncoming cat missed us by inches, and I mean inches! I could see that there was no one aboard and recognized the boat. It was one of the twenty-one boats that I found out later had blown out of the next bay. This one had missed running onto the three barrier islands or the reefs that protected that bay. It had passed over the giant breaking waves or slipped out the tiny pass and made its way down the island, turned, and entered the bay at Le Galion...unmanned! And it had missed colliding with us by inches. It had now disappeared into the white, and within fifteen minutes debris of a shipwreck started blowing by.

I took a compass bearing of where it went so as NOT to go there and plotted a course for the beach. I was for sure moving and I sure as hell didn't want to be blown out to sea. Well, that is exactly what happened...five times! Even powering full into 175 knots of wind I was slowly going backwards and out into twenty-five-foot perfect surf—except the offshore breeze was a little more than we normally liked to see.

Knowing that as soon as we got into those breaking waves we were going to capsize, I prepared the boat for that eventuality. We stowed all the loose gear, put on our harnesses and life jackets, sent a message out on the VHF radio, and brought the bedding up into the deckhouse for padding and floatation. But as *Shadowfax* went backwards up these mountains of waves, 115 horses going full tilt boogie and me steering a compass course for the beach, she would break into a surf, outrun the wave, and shoot back into the bay. Then the fifteen feet of white water and foam would catch up. Michelle would yell, "Wave!" and I would dive into the deckhouse, slamming the doors behind me as a wall of water washed over us, sending the boat nearly...and I say nearly...onto the beach. Then the slow backward battle out to the surf line would start again.

What a great boat! By three p.m. we had ridden our second wave back inside. It actually got clear for about thirty minutes and I thought the storm was abating.... but nooooooo that was far from the truth. And I had noticed at the end of our second surf that we were nearing the other end of the bay far from where we had departed. There was nothing there but rocks, an eighty-foot piece of rocky, pebbly, sandy beach with a small concrete house next to it on the road, and "The Needle," a quarter-mile-long point of rocks twenty to thirty feet high with waves breaking over it.

Out we went again. This time as we surfed back in, we lost the prop as it hit the reef. The hulls were still intact, but we were now out of control. We prepared again to capsize. I even kissed the boat goodbye. I told Michelle that one of us was sure to die on this one and it would not be her. I told her how much I loved her and that the Boy Scout in me would save her life. And in we came...OVER the boulders, past the road, past the house, past the power line poles, and back out and didn't touch a thing.

That is when we decided to jump. On the next pass we reckoned, as the boat washed to a stop and before going out on its fourth trip, we would leap off the boat and take refuge in that little concrete house by the road. We prepared to abandon ship. Life jackets were inflated and we life-lined ourselves together. I attached my harness also to the calamity or ditch bag that held water, first aid, food, passports, a hand-held VHF radio, ship's papers, and what little money we had left. As we surfed in, Michelle and I inched our way out on the bow. We again went past the house, past the road, past the power line poles; stopped, and just before we washed back out...we missed the jump! The ditch bag that was tied to me hung up on something and I was tied to Michelle, and dammit to hell, we missed the jump!

Backwards with a whoosh and a bang we went as the boat hit the house at the corner of its roof. We heard a wood-splintering crash and knew that now there was a hole in the boat. Then just to add insult to injury, the other corner of the roof grabbed the starboard rigging and ripped it out of the deck. Now the masts were going to fall. I yelled to Michelle to get inside the protection of the deckhouse as I quickly travelled the two booms over to the far end of the starboard traveler and sheeted them tight on a winch. This effectively acted as backstays and that held the rigs up. Then I too dived inside.

The rigs held as we spun out for a fifth surf back in. This time we washed up upon a huge mound of seaweed that had accumulated throughout the day, cushioning our landing, and we stopped on something. We just stopped and were hung up on something. The waves still washed in and picked us up, but we stayed there head to wind, flying a hull from time to time—eight times, actually. But we were not going anywhere. Michelle still wanted to make the jump and get into the little house, but we seemed safe enough right where we lay except for the hull flying, of course. So we stayed put and a good thing too, because by the next day…That house was not there!

Now mind you, the storm was not over yet. It was sunset now. The doors to the deckhouse had disappeared sometime in the last two surfs. The roof of the house had left a huge hole in the starboard lazarette, and all the starboard side rigging was flying in the breeze. The dinghy had been torn from its davits and was nowhere to be seen. The davits themselves were a twisted piece of stainless steel sculpture. When that happened I had no recollection. But we, of all things, were still alive.

Champagne? Did anyone say champagne? Should we pop a bottle of bubbly? We had been fighting this storm all day and the bottle, a little shaken, was still cold. Michelle, God bless her, asked if it was not a wee bit premature, to which I responded that if it was, we were gonna be dead later so we might as well drink it now, now, now! That was a sunset I will always remember. Twelve hours of fighting a storm, and here we were drinking champagne. Upon finishing the bottle we did what most heroes do during a lull in a battle, we passed out.

I had seen and surfed waves that seemed like mountains. I had seen a thirty-six-foot trimaran blow over backwards. I had seen a boat flash by just to disintegrate in the white. I had seen whole roofs flying by like Frisbees and an animal—dog or goat, I could not tell which—blow by overhead. I had sailed ashore past where cars drive, hit a house with my boat, and above all, I had lost a fingernail…we passed out.

It was the quiet that woke me up. One thirty a.m. Wednesday morning on the sixth and I woke up to no wind and stars. Wispy clouds were sauntering overhead and I realized that it was the eye, just the eye. Now what were we gonna do? In a very short time we were going to have two hundred mile per hour gusts blowing in the opposite direction right into the deckhouse and I had no doors. Why, that would make that deckhouse blow down the road quicker than an empty shoe-box. I immediately jumped off the boat and began to scour the beach for some piece of something to cover the open doorway. I found an entire piece of three-quarter-inch plywood not far away and walked with it back to the boat to find that it fit perfectly. Taking out my trusty cordless drill and dipping into my supply of sheet metal screws, I securely fastened the ply over the opening and then entered the aft cabin's deck hatch, dogged it down, and waited for the wind to blow. Sure enough, within thirty minutes it started that god awful shrieking again.

All dark morning long it howled, slinging rocks and debris and animals and shit at us until eight a.m. We did not move an inch! Man, we were so far from the water after the wind changed that there was no way in hell that storm was gonna blow us back into the sea!

After twenty-four hours the storm started to abate, and finally we could see with the daylight exactly what a major hurricane could do. And I had thought that the hurricane in Kauai, Iniki, was bad. This was worse, waaayyy worse. There was nothing left. No roofs, no windows, no nothing. All that was left of that little con-crete house we were going to take refuge in was the toilet, and all the shit from its septic tank was in the hulls of the boat. Just imagine it, septic mud and a ton of seaweed, corals, sponges, and, of all things, dead hummingbirds, HUMMINGBIRDS, hundreds of them filling the hulls. I surmised that when the trees all blow away there never really is something birds can hang onto, now is there?

There we were, sitting on this mound of seaweed and debris high and dry. I ventured out to survey the situation and found a twisted lump of rubber, fiberglass, and debris, which was my dinghy, at the end of the little beach. Debris was everywhere. I noticed that hanging off the bow roller of my boat were parted anchor rodes and...my mooring, I was still on my mooring! That hundred-pound Danforth was bent double and the fluke pointing in opposing directions and fouled with coral, wire, rock, and who knows what.

Now that would explain the slow drag out to sea, and the surfs back into the bay. As the boat went up the face of the waves the mooring would come off the bottom and the cat would take off on its spectacular surfs. With the boat buoyed by the extra twenty feet of water in the bay, the mooring would not touch down until we arrived quite near the beach. Then it would try to reattach itself to the bottom, but with 175 knots of offshore breeze, the boat would stay head to wind and then would drag that mooring slowly back out to the surf zone and everything would start again.

After securing the boat and setting up another camp, we went into shipwreck survival mode. An Aussie friend Bruce, whose boat ended up on the bottom of the lagoon along with over nine hundred other yachts, came along and offered to help me rebuild *Shadowfax* if he could live aboard. I invited him in. The three of us in three days jacked up the boat level using a hydraulic mast ram from a wrecked race boat. Bruce put up a sign: "Abbo Boat Works," commemorating aboriginal Australian boat building technology as we had no power and only hand tools and had to rebuild the old way.

Shadowfax was 119 feet from the water's edge. One hull rested on the sand and stone. That was the hull that had flown, and upon its landing, the rocks had knocked nine holes through to the interior. The other hull, as I had mentioned, was resting on a huge mound of seaweed that housed, well, covered, of all things, a bulldozer! It had pierced that hull quite well and held us fast as the waves pounded us and the other hull flew. I had been held in place by my mooring and a bulldozer. Thanks for small miracles.

I wondered what had happened to my four anchors and wanted to salvage one or two if I could find them to use after our eventual launching. A slow snorkel following the scar on the bottom of the bay left by the dragging mooring answered that question. They were right where I had placed them. I kept swimming along the snaking scar, sticking my head up from time to time exclaiming,"Wow, we were here!" and "Oh my God, we were HERE!" All the way to the point of departure I snorkeled and marveled at the amount of debris that the lobsters had already moved under. There were lobster, fish, and stingrays everywhere such as I had not seen in twenty years. It was surreal.

When I finally came to the anchorage and the upturned *Tryst,* I found my rudders right where I had left them. They were surrounded by four-by-four pieces of timber ten to fifteen feet long lodged in the bottom like javelins. If we had stayed in that protected spot, that timber would have skewered us. It had all belonged to a hotel of bungalows a mile to windward that had been disintegrated by the winds. All of them save for the only one that had housed any people—the hotel manager and his dog. So you see there is a God. And what about my anchors, you may ask? Well, the two on the sandbar were well dug in and right where I had left them, one on the beach was just too deep to retrieve, and the other when I dug it up had two Indonesian gardeners attached claiming possession. You see, in the West Indies when you dig a hole it is not to China but to Indonesia, which is on the other side of the world. And it was the debris flying by at two hundred miles per hour that had severed my anchor rode and sent me on the ride of my life!

Luis left us and went "safety out to sea." The lighthouse keeper on Sombrero Rock, north of St. Maarten, reported waves washing over the island at fifty-five feet of elevation. They had had to abandon their stone house and run for the protection of the tower. Swaying too much to ascend and too flooded for them to depart, they spent their horrific twenty-four hours on the stairs as waves again and again passed over the island. On September 11, the cruise ship *QE II,* traversing the North Atlantic, was stopped dead in the water at four o'clock a.m. as a wave measuring one hundred feet washed over her pilot house and bridge.

St. Maarten was devastated. Seventy percent of all structures were destroyed and there were nine reported deaths, all yachtsmen and women in their boats. Two thousand yachts were wrecked with over nine hundred sunk. Six were unscathed, twenty-one were floating. A reported $1.8 billion of damage was incurred. The United States Navy, flying relief from

Puerto Rico, reported that St. Maarten was easy to find, just follow the debris trail floating in the sea all the way to the island.

As for my loss, *Shadowfax* was repaired in two months and launched all by hand, "abbo ingenuity," and help from my friends. Sadly, Michelle who I had met in 1989 and Hurricane Hugo, who had ventured with me into Kauai and Iniki in 1992, and now had weathered a deadly sail in Luis, left me. She told me in no uncertain terms that my life had just become way too adventurous for her. But who's to blame her, eh?

A bird's eye view of my hurricane hole at Le Galion, St. Martin. Note the absence of any hotel after the storm. Shadowfax *started her journey in the bottom left-hand corner of the bay behind the headland, went out into the waves, and ended the ordeal on the tiny beach just visible at the top left corner of the photo.*

Shadowfax *shipwrecked. The rectangular holes at the stern of the boat are the repairs being made after she hit the roof of a house. The telephone pole in the upper right-hand corner was the one we sailed by before we hit the house! The debris in front of the boat is what is left of the house.*

Sailboats line the entire perimeter of Simpson Bay's lagoon after the devastation wreaked by Hurricane Luis in September 1995. Of the almost two thousand boats on the island, only six in the lagoon remained unscathed.

Before Luis arrived full force, he was preceded by a huge swell. Bobby's Marina, Great Bay, St. Maarten.

After 24 hours of waves and 200 mph wind, Luis left a tale to tell. Bobby's Marina, Great Bay, St. Maarten.

Chapter 14

To Find a Safe Haven

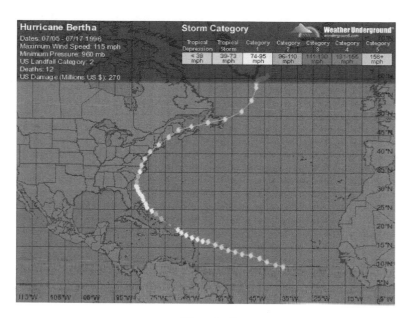

"Bertha"
July 10, 1996

It is amazing how time flies. *Shadowfax,* a newly rebuilt cat, has taken me through the tough time of post traumatic stress and the little bit of tourism in the Caribbean due to the hurricanes of the season before. But I made it and, like a bad dream, June 1 was upon me and the National Hurricane Center Miami was once again on line. "Run away, run away!" began pounding in my mind. But where to go and what to do was the dilemma. It wasn't safe anywhere in the Caribbean, it seemed to me, and for some foolish reason I picked the Bahamas.

I had spent my young, impressionable years in the Bahamas. I used to hitchhike out there via plane or banana boat and spent months on end surfing and spear fishing. My first sailing trip was on a twenty-eight-foot Erickson from Hatchet Bay, Eleuthera, to Gregorytown, Eleuthera, a trip of about eleven miles, and we had motored the entire way. That sowed the seed of yachting in my blood, and darn if I could ever remember a hurricane passing there. Of course I had only been sixteen years old, but what the heh.

In the Abacos, the most northern islands in the Bahamas, my sister had a place on the canals of Treasure Cay and I chose to sail *Shadowfax* up there from St. Barth. I was off with two friends for a summer in the Bahamas. Having a great sail up, four days under a spinnaker after a respite in the U.S. Virgin Islands, brought us right up through the archipelago. I should have taken a warning when I noticed a storm-wrecked yacht on the beach at Aucklin Island, but we jibed away and continued northwest.

My second heads up came when finally approaching the Abacos from the ocean. We were caught up in a sixty-knot squall just at the entrance to the cut. Sails down and still sailing at ten knots and visibility nil we lay a-hull just outside the entrance between the reefs as the mini tempest passed. There I changed my pants.

Shoot, I said, welcome to the Bahamas. But by July 8 my superstitious fear subsided as on line I saw that Hurricane Bertha, an early Cape Verde storm, had formed and was threatening the Leeward Islands. On the ninth I receive the coordinates of the storm: eighteen degrees north, sixty-three degrees west or 1.2 nautical miles southeast of Phillipsburg, St. Maarten. Damn, was this storm looking for me too? I swiped the sweat off my forehead, breathed a sigh of relief, and calmed down...until four days later.

Now what are the chances of the eye of that storm, which had just passed directly over the islands on which I lived, coming over me here in the Bahamas? No way José, I was thinking, and once again I was proven wrong. Yes, four days later and four days stronger, Bertha was Bahamas bound!

My son, sister, and I were racing a Conser forty-two-foot catamaran during Abaco Race Week when everyone got the news. A hurricane was coming and it was coming here and it was coming here tomorrow! Not winning a thing in the regatta, we opted to jump on the "*Fax*" now moored in Marsh Harbor on Great Abaco, skip the awards presentation, and head for home at Treasure Cay twelve miles down the pike. The wind being light, as in the "calm before the storm," we motored down the coast of Great Abaco checking out

Leisure Lee, a man-made canal-infused undeveloped development along the way. Although protected from the storm's surge, the canals were enveloped on both sides by casuarinas trees. These are bear-like looking pines, wispy in nature, whose trunks are strong enough to tie onto but whose root systems are notoriously shallow, giving them a propensity to fall over in high winds.

The canals of Treasure Cay seemed safer as my sister Sandy knew of a dock we could lash to. In the Bahamas, the wind is usually not the destroyer, I was told, but rather the surge. The ocean comes right over the islands, and if you are not moored correctly and tied to very tall pilings you would float right off of them and then you are really in the shit. Sandy's Bahamian friend had such a dock with high piles on a canal behind his house. We snuck *Shadowfax* into his canal, just squeaking by a hairpin sandbank turn, and came up alongside the dock. Tall pilings, they said, these were over twelve feet tall. We roped off to them plus spider-webbed lines across the canal and dove in three anchors to the stern of the boat. We were not going anywhere. Once again I stowed the sails and ran the halyards up the mast and this time took off the wind vane instrument that reported wind speed. During Luis I found out that it only reports to sixty knots of wind, and after 140 knots, it just goes away! Warping the boat off the dock and in the center of the canal, we secured the new dinghy to the new davits and battened down the ship to wait it out.

The sea came right over the island, sure enough. There was no housing damage, as those Bahamians knew how to build for a hurricane. The casuarinas trees that for the longest time looked like dancing bears fell down, and sand and fish found their way into the houses but we hardly rocked. What a safe haven. And the eye passed ten miles to weather, directly over Green Turtle Cay. The trees got it there too. The storm continued on to landfall at Wilmington, N.C., and also did its damage there. For us, well, the day after we were windsurfing and for me, happy to be alive...but that nagging question remained in my mind...were these nasty things truly following me around?

Chapter 15

Run Away and Enjoy the Ride

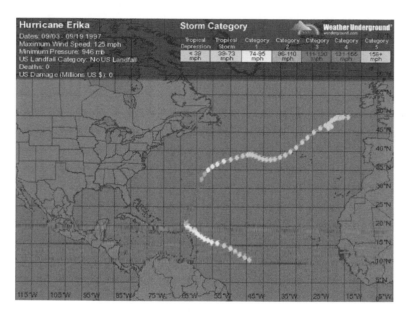

Hurricane Erika
Dates: 09/03 - 09/19 1997
Maximum Wind Speed: 125 mph
Minimum Pressure: 946 mb
US Landfall Category: No US Landfall
Deaths: 0
US Damage (Millions US $): 0

Storm Category

Weather Underground

Tropical Depression	Tropical Storm	Category 1	Category 2	Category 3	Category 4	Category 5
< 39 mph	39-73 mph	74-95 mph	96-110 mph	111-130 mph	131-155 mph	156+ mph

"Erika"
September 8, 1997

B ack to the West Indies we went. There was just no getting away from these storms. Another storm, another Dean, brushed the Bahamas in '96 but caused no damage, and although we prepared in the canals of Treasure Cay for the onslaught, it was hardly worth mentioning. After its passing I put together a delivery crew and we departed into a leftover sea. So confused it was that on the first day everyone was seasick! On the second day the birds started showing up. Little buggers who had been carried to sea in the fury of the winds started landing tired and featherless on the deck of *Shadowfax* for a rest. On the fourth day out we even had a red-tailed hawk drop in for a respite and we were five hundred miles out! No wonder all the hummingbirds died off in Luis on St. Maarten in '95. Birds and high winds just don't mix.

As the '97 hurricane season approached I paid intense attention to the National Hurricane Center Miami on the Internet. Every morning with a cup of coffee I started my daily routine with checking the weather. My plan for my stalkers was to...run away!

Shadowfax can easily sail nineteen to twenty knots, and if a storm were to approach from the east as per usual, I would simply head south. As I had learned from all the yachts that had survived Luis in '95, it gets windy and out of the north it blows, the seas get large, but you are sailing away from the eye of a storm. Let it blow forty knots, it is blowing 140 knots from where you departed!

And that is exactly what Anne Lynn, my new girl-friend, Curly, my partner in crime, and I did for Erika as she threatened St. Barth. We ran away. We provisioned the boat as soon as the National Hurricane Center forecast St. Barth to be in the center of their cone of probability...the storm could hit the Northern Antilles in three days. By the eighth of September the storm would be seventy-five nautical miles east of St. Barth. We were to be 250 nautical miles south. As soon as the light southerlies switched to the north, as it does in every approaching storm, we blew out of there. Running at ten knots down island means we would be making at least 240 miles every twenty-four hours. I remember Curly asking if we should put a reef in the sails as the northerly wind built from fifteen to twenty-five to thirty knots, and the sixty-foot cat was surfing down the mounting swells at eighteen knots. "Shoots no," I responded. "Run away, run away!" I now had a built-in respect and, yes, fear of hurricanes and I wanted out of their way!

We ran all day, all night, and all day, until the wind quit as Erika passed just to the north of the islands of St. Barth, St. Maarten/St. Martin, and Anguilla. Then we hung a left and stopped at the first island we saw, this time the island being Martinique. Sailing into Fort de France on a dying westerly we anchored in the bay on the town's waterfront and went in to celebrate...it was the ninth of September and my birthday.

As we dinghied in, I noted a Morgan 50 named *Dare* in the anchorage. It used to belong to my old friend "Action Jackson." Stopping to say hello, we found that it had been purchased by Captain Will and his wife. He was the captain of Tom Hill's *Titan 11* and I had skippered *Titan 3*. I had known Will since passing him in the Panama Canal when he was the skip on *Sea Angle* and I was delivering the catamaran *Spirit of Kauai* out to the Hawaiian Islands to replace Captain Andy's cat lost in Hurricane Iniki. On board *Dare*, Will's wife was alone with their new, and I mean brand-new, baby, and oddly enough the wife was chatting with Captain Will via the SSB radio. Small world or what?

Giving our fond hellos and asking if she needed anything, she confided that some baby formula would be great, so Curly and I went ashore and procured a case. Then the next day, the wind switched as per usual out of the south and began to blow. The harbor turned into a rock and roll maelstrom and the yachts in the moorage were going wild. All except *Shadowfax,* that is. Being a catamaran her motion was quite level and comfortable. But *Dare* looked to be untenable. Rolling gunnels to gunnels accompanied by wild pitch tugging at her two anchors looked unbearable, so Curly and I zoomed over to offer assistance. Poor Mrs. Captain Will, poor baby! We took them both back to *Shadowfax* for a calm evening and a feed for the baby.

The next day the wind abated a little and the anchorage grew calmer. Calm enough to let the fledgling family back aboard *Dare*. Then again with the wind behind us, we sailed back to St. Barth. Passing the island of Montserrat, we got to see a spectacular light show as the volcano began erupting in the night. We were so close to the island that I remember seeing white cliffs, ones I had never seen before, and upon peering through my binoculars I realized that they were not cliffs at all but STEAM! A pyroclastic flow was tumbling down the mountain at about one hundred miles per hour and the heat and ash were dumping into the sea not one hundred yards beside us! Run away, run away, and we tacked off toward Guadeloupe. Then with a squall line between us and that island, the full moon poked its bright head through and we witnessed a moon bow…Yes, a moonbow, not a rainbow but similar and at night and caused by the light of the moon. And it was white…white, white, and white. To add to the amazement, it doubled up and we saw a DOUBLE moonbow! What a treat.

The following morning we arrived at our point of departure, Gustavia, St. Barth, to a mess. One yacht sunk in the harbor, others on the rocks. After securing the "*Fax*" to the quay we immediately got to work helping the clean-up and listening to hurricane stories that we were not privy to…thank God. From then on, I swore that if I had a yacht in the National Hurricane Center's cone of probability of a hurricane strike, I would run away…and enjoy the ride.

Chapter 16

Land Bound and Swimming

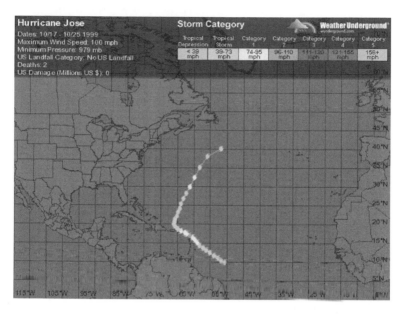

Hurricane Jose
Dates: 10/17 - 10/25 1999
Maximum Wind Speed: 100 mph
Minimum Pressure: 979 mb
US Landfall Category: No US Landfall
Deaths: 2
US Damage (Millions US $): 0

"Jose"
October 21, 1999

I ran away a lot in 1998, finally leaving my boat hauled out on the island of Grenada for the duration of the hurricane season of '99. Rumor had it that hurricanes never—well, not at least in the last thirty-five years—hit Grenada, and insurance companies were clamoring for its clients to pass the season there or points farther south.

I had also taken a land job, the first in a long, long, time: Care-taking the old Rockefeller estate in St. Barth, and it was a super interesting job, also my first time land-bound since David and Florida in 1979. David and Peggy Rockefeller had built a family retreat on ninety-six hectares of land in 1959. It was the family survival compound in the event that the nuclear balloons went up. Totally self-contained and separated from the main part of the island, the estate had its own power plant, desalination system that produced twenty thousand liters of water a day, and gardens that at one time were planted with all types of vegetables. Cattle and geese were farmed. Not to mention that, to intercept Russian submarine communications with their spy trawlers, a secret CIA radio listening base was hidden under the guesthouse. It was its own microcosm.

The house was Frank Lloyd Wright-ish, what I would call modern medieval, and designed by his protégés, Fischer and Payne, Boston. Completely built of stone, the walls were up to four feet thick. Poured concrete roof and bronze-framed windows housed 12mm plate glass. The structure was a sculpture of a bomb shelter if there ever was one. The property was totally irrigated and we had just planted fifty-two full-grown coconut trees to replace the long-gone grove that had existed in the '60s. The entire estate was a water catchments system: roofs, roads, parking, decks, all ran off into six-inch drains that led to six fifteen thousand-gallon cisterns. The water was then purified through five industrial-sized composite filters and run through twelve pumps to supply the house and gardens. What a place...what a job! An enclave only accessible by foot, boat, or helicopter, built by the United States Army Corps of Engineers and the labor of St. Barth, it was a surreal property right out of a James Bond novel.

Living on the estate and bringing it back to working condition became my main project. Thus on the fifteenth of October I took notice of a strong tropical wave making its way across the Atlantic from the African coast. By the seventeenth it was a tropical depression and the next day...Tropical Storm Jose. Four hundred nautical miles off the coast of the Lesser Antilles, Jose became, on the nineteenth, a hurricane and it was time to get ready for landfall—St. Barth. By October 20, the storm had a central pressure of 979mb and the eye was over Antigua and the wind speed was maxing at eighty-nine knots. Not too dangerous really, but I had battened down the hatches anyway.

The estate had three boats that I had to deal with plus two cars and a truck. The property also included a dock in town dubbed the "Rock Dock" that had an apartment and a garage that housed a classic 1979 VW Thing and a stock of South American hardwoods from Laurence's farms in Venezuela. One of the boats, the Boston Whaler, was hauled out and put alongside the car, and then the garage and adjoining apartment had to be boarded up. I had plenty of wood for that. The second boat, a vintage 1960 Blue Point Lobsterman, was hauled out on its own classic, hand-built hardwood trailer and lashed to tree trunks as well as tie downs imbedded in the concrete. I took the third boat back out to the estate, wound it up on its davits on the quay, and tied her off to keep the rising water from floating her away.

Alone now on the property, I set to boarding up the windows with specially made covers that bolted into the bronze frames, but with the storm being only eighty-nine knots or so and the windows being bulletproof I left off that chore and nailed plywood over the office windows as well as the ones on the servant's quarters. I parked the truck in the garage on the quay and boarded the doors up well. The last vehicle, an old Renault van that the president of France, Jacques Chirac, had ridden around in on his visit to the island, was placed on the old helipad, far from flying debris or falling trees.

I then secured all the entrances to the house using the kitchen door as my egress. I was prepared, so let it howl! On a calm day the Rockefeller House is windy. It keeps it cool in the summer. However, when I say howl, it screamed, "howl!" After my experience of Hurricane Luis in '95, I hated it when it screamed and the post traumatic stress disorder took over and I flipped out!

It drove me so crazy that I locked up the house and walked out just like that. It was blowing fifty knots and the seas were breaking up the cliffs and I took a thirty-minute hike out and along them. There is nothing like being a fool and nature walking during a hurricane. As I neared the end of the hiking trail and the beginning of the road, I got coverage on my cell phone and gave a good friend of mine, Laurent, a call and asked if I could pass the hurricane with him. You see, Laurent lives in a proper "case à vent" (pronounced cause-a-vont), a concrete bunker of a house situated on the southeast coast of the island, a place called Point Toiny. And traditionally the cases à vent were built by the islanders who lived on the windward side of the island to withstand wind, any kind of wind, and in it I would feel safe.

Laurent picked me up at the road's end and whisked me away to his side of the island, berating me the entire way. I was being foolish, after all, to leave a nuclear bomb shelter and go for a hike in a storm just because of a little wind. But to the Villa Rose we went. There, overlooking the beach and point, we stood in the lee of one of the walls of the house and watched Jose unwind, or wind up, I should say. Waves became huge, breaking a quarter of a mile out to sea. Oddly enough they were passing beyond the bight at the point. One could have safely anchored a yacht there up until the full fury of the storm was unleashed. An amazing sight really.

Bits of roof started flying by after a while, yet no rain, just wind. It was like an invisible hand was picking things up and making them fly, almost magical. I was mesmerized, lulled into a sense of security. We were awakened from our reverie when a sea grape leaf slapped Laurent upside the head at about fifty miles per hour and just stuck there. It was time to retire into the redoubt of the concrete case and double pin the storm shutters, so in we went.

These shutters are made of wood and three inches thick. They close up the house like a fortress. Well, it was howling out now and those damn shutters kept on bowing in during the gusts. I tell you, I was scared. And then the phone rang! Rang, I tell you; in this entire maelstrom and howl the phone was still working and it rang. Well, it was a friend of ours, T.K. in Antigua, the island ninety miles to the east of us, telling us that the eye of Jose had passed there and was heading our way. He gave us the coordinates of the center and I realized that position was approximately right outside this house...Well, give or take a few miles. We took a peek out and there was still not a drop of rain as yet. Now that was odd. Looking out to sea, I could make out a grey wall, sort of fog-like and near the shore, perhaps three or four miles out. As it got closer I came to the conclusion that this grey wall was not a fog or a squall line but seawater, and it was blowing sideways at one hundred miles per hour. This water was being picked up and blown sideways by the same invisible hand, the wind. *Ominous, frightening, mind-blowing* were words that come to mind.

And then Jose hit. Now there was no phone, no power, just shriek and howl and that was bugging the shit out of me. I remember seeing videos of Hurricane Luis three years after the event and I would break into tears. I swore then that I would never be in another storm and here I was again. The storm shutters were bowing in, debris was rattling off the house walls and roof, there was driving rain...I went to bed, put the covers over my head, and tried to sleep. I tried rum when sleep failed, ganja when rum failed, and hash when the ganja failed. The hash did me in...Thank God!

I woke up to rain, lots of rain, tons of rain. It rained buckets, barrels, cats, dogs, frogs; it rained so much it flooded the pig farm down on the beach and the pigs swam OVER the fences. It rained so hard that whole roads washed away. The St. Barth family Ledee had land washed down the mountain on to the family Magras land (now that was a lawsuit in the making). The capital of St. Barth, Gustavia, lost its upper road and for four more years, if it rained, cars could not mount the other two exits because the roads were too steep, too slippery, and too wet. Water ran into town for three months after the storm and there was a waterfall down the cliffs near "Rockefeller" that tumbled for eight days. If a bare boating couple had sailed in, an argument would have ensued as to which island this was. You see, only Dominica has a waterfall visible from the sea…the cruising guide says so!

It rained seventy-two centimeters in forty-eight hours, and mud and displaced land was everywhere. I even drove into town over the mountain at Lurin only to find my return path blocked one minute after by a huge bolder crashing onto the road blocking all passage. A friend of mine in Grand Fond had a boulder the size of a dump truck land in his swimming pool and the pool was so new that he had not even put water in it yet! The road to the estate on Gouveneur Plage no longer existed. The road to St. Jean was chest deep in water. In Lorient we found freshwater crayfish on the beach washed down from the mountain, and there is no source of fresh water up the mountain! Maybe it even rained crayfish!

At Laurent's house we diverted water for five hours with rakes, Squeegees, and mops to keep it from flooding the interior. Up the hill the neighbor's house had water running out of the windows. When we opened its doors we released a cascade onto Laurent's house below. Only Herculean effort on Laurent's part saved his humble abode from flooding. There was also a new river mouth on the beach where the pig farm used to be. There was no sign of the pigs. After drying out, I decided to head over the hill and take a boat out to "Rockefeller."

Arriving at the "Rock Dock," I found no damage at all. It was just muddy in the streets. I pulled the Whaler out of the garage, launched her, and headed out to the property. From out at sea one was really awed by the extent of rain that had fallen. There were landslides everywhere, not just the road in town, but three more could be viewed on the way out. The road at Columbier, overlooking Anse Gastogne, had slid to the sea. There were new rocky beaches and small waterfalls all along the cliffs. There was the aforementioned cascade at "Rockefeller" that simply blew my mind.

But upon arriving at the estate there seemed to be…nothing. Oh, a coconut had flown through the windshield of the president's van, but that seemed about the extent of it all. The garage was intact, the truck and desalination plant in fine shape. Power was out, but that happened anytime it rained. Trekking up to the main house I noticed that the cistern under the gardener's house was overflowing and the road was a running stream but the catchments had done their job. And they had done it all too well.

Walking into the main house I noticed that the water had flowed through it and had made a mess in the TV room. The wooden floors were heaped up like a wooden wave as the water and mud had undermined the foundation. Out of the front window I could see that the road across the property to the beach had disappeared, leaving a gaping hole lined with curbs. Not good. A few of the coconut palms had been washed over, but that would be no big deal to rectify. But something else bothered me. Where had all the water gone?

Upon entering the basement and wine cellar I got my answer. It was neck deep in water! It seemed that the six-inch intakes at all the catchments worked perfectly but the four-inch overflows did not, and the drains backed up, flooding the entire house. Then the water ran down the stairs into the cellar where floating debris had clogged the one drain. Here I was situated on top of a hill standing in a house that was flooded. In I went for a swim to find the drain and unclog it. Utilizing a mask and snorkel I rummaged around underwater until I could find the plugged orifice. Removing a mishmash of cardboard, paper, and whatnot, the water began to subside. The damage became evident: the power boxes and transformer that converts 220volts to 110 volts had been under water, and the deep freeze, the refrigerators, all the pumps that ran the mechanics of the estate were ruined.

You get the picture: all was lost. And do you think we had flood insurance, on an island that barely had water, for a house that sat on top of a hill? Well, noooooo, of course not. Shoots, the whole island didn't have flood insurance; hurricane insurance, yes, but this catastrophe happened AFTER the storm had passed. That is what the insurance people would say. What a mess upon a mess.

All one could do was to dry out. Which is exactly what I did, along with putting hydrogen peroxide and alcohol in my ears because, after all, how many times does one get to go swimming on land...or on a hill... in a cellar in a house?

You Lookin' For Me?

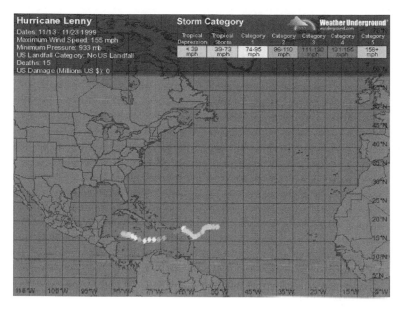

Hurricane Lenny
Dates: 11/13 - 11/23 1999
Maximum Wind Speed: 155 mph
Minimum Pressure: 933 mb
US Landfall Category: No US Landfall
Deaths: 15
US Damage (Millions US $): 0

Storm Category

Tropical Depression	Tropical Storm	Category 1	Category 2	Category 3	Category 4	Category 5
< 39 mph	39-73 mph	74-95 mph	96-110 mph	111-130 mph	131-155 mph	156+ mph

Weather Underground

"Lenny"
November 16–19, 1999

According to Commodore Munroe: Biscayne Bay, 1877

JUNE–TOO SOON

JULY–STAND BY

AUGUST–LOOK OUT YOU MUST

SEPTEMBER–REMEMBER

OCTOBER–ALL OVER

It was November when Hurricane Lenny came to hunt around the islands for yours truly. I had made the mistake of flying to Grenada and launching *Shadowfax* and sailed her back up to St. Barth. It was the last month of hurricane season, by the way, and we had already had our hurricane for the year. What chance was there to have another one? Our little French island was drying out from the deluge of Jose. The waterfalls were subsiding, the basement at "Rockefeller" was dry, and the electrics had been replaced. Power was on; the pumps were repaired and running. The cisterns were full!

A fifty-year anniversary marked the halfway days between the end of Jose and the beginning of Lenny. In the capital of St. Barth, Gustavia, Le Select, the famous pirate bar belonging to the ancient Swedish family of Marius, was having a birthday and all of the Caribbean sailors were flocking to this "sunny place for shady characters." Jimmy brought his entire band and held a free concert on the quay. The harbor was packed, a party ensued.

November 12 and a hurricane hunter was sent into a disturbance far in the western Caribbean. You see, toward the beginning and the end of hurricane season, early and then late season storms tend to develop in the western Caribbean and Gulf of Mexico and then travel ashore somewhere along the Gulf's coastline. A lump of rain and wind had formed and was sitting off the coast of Central America and Mexico. By the thirteenth it had become better organized and we were thinking, oh the poor Gulf Coast, they are going to get a late season storm. Around Le Select, the party continued.

Jimmy and the band left, the party finished, all the champagne corks collected down by the desalination intake at "Rockefeller," and the sailors and yachts had all gone home. Good thing too because by the fourteenth we had Tropical Storm Lenny, and for the first time in the history of hurricane reporting, this storm started moving east! The damn thing was gusting to eighty-four knots and with a central pressure of 988mb. I kept a watchful eye out. Being as how I had just brought *Shadowfax* up from Granada and the tourist season was about to be upon us, I had an extra boat to look after. Even though the chances were slim that the storm would come our way, I was on guard. I had already learned through Hurricane Chris in 1994 to keep a sharp lookout over my shoulder and to expect the unexpected. After all, the only thing predictable about hurricanes is that they are unpredictable.

Reading every morning the National Hurricane Center's storm report on the Internet, I was torn between a false sense of security and a bad gut feeling. The center predicted the storm to pass over Jamaica on the fifteenth, but by the sixteenth Lenny was still 150 nautical miles south of the Cayman Islands and still moving east. The storm was now a hurricane with consistent wind speeds of eighty-five knots and a central pressure of 978mb. On the morning of the seventeenth, after a predicated turn to the north over Haiti, no, the Dominican Republic, no, Puerto Rico, the storm was eighteen nautical miles south of St. Croix, blowing 135 knots, the central pressure had dropped to 933mb, and it was now, after a short drift northeast, heading south-southeast! Time to move it, move it, and move it!

All day the seventeenth I prepared the house. With winds to 135 knots, Lenny was a dangerous threat so this time I bolted on the storm covers over the plate glass windows at the house. Closing off the cistern intakes and closing up the estate as I had for Jose, I put the small boat on its davits and hiked into town. The Lobsterman was still hauled out and I pulled out the Whaler and put it into the garage next to the VW Thing. All day it took me and this time I had help. I had called a friend of mine, a stunningly beautiful woman named Dot who had skippered and crewed on the catamarans from St. Maarten for fifteen years. She was visiting friends on St. Barth when the fiftieth anniversary started and was now on the island as Lenny was threatening. She, like me, did not want to weather a storm on land, no way José! Opting to assist me, she said she would help me sail *Shadowfax* south and out of harm's way no matter what the weather.

Yachts were skedaddling all day with some going to the safety of St. Maarten's lagoon while others, like *Mischievous,* the sixty-five-foot Meriten race boat, headed for Guadeloupe. I told the captain, Mark Del, that I would be right behind. Dot and I provisioned *Shadowfax* and by sunset we were out of there. A little late in leaving but we got out of there anyway.

The strange thing is that for the first time in history we were experiencing a hurricane coming from the opposite direction. It started the same, a calm before the storm, and we motored off toward Guadeloupe in a no wind situation.

The wind after a while filled in out of the south and not the normal northerly direction and began to build. We had motored past ten other yachts before we started to sail. Falling off onto a port tack we were zooming along at twelve knots heading for the north side of Montserrat, a British island one hundred nautical miles to weather. The night turned ominous black and we engaged the autopilot and continued to beat into a building gale.

Between sunset and midnight the wind picked up to forty knots. I had a small jib and a reefed mizzen flying, meaning I had a tiny triangle of a sail in the front of the boat and half the behind sail set on the behind mast. The mainsail was doused and furled tight. We were still making ten knots and, though a bit wet, were comfortably making ground on the storm. Lenny, it seems, had slowed its forward motion, and by the eighteenth would end up wandering around St. Maarten/St. Martin, Anguilla, St. Barth, and St. Kitts as we pounded our way south. By two a.m. on the eighteenth, we were thumping along in a building sea. The radio forecast seas to twelve meters...*meters,* for chrissake! That is over twenty-four feet! And the fore-casted wind was to 130 knots.

Well, we were not up there in the center of the forecast area, but where we were was bad enough. About three-dark-thirty, Dot came out of the deck-house to give me a cup of coffee when she remarked with excitement, "What the fuck is that!" Yes, that sweetheart of a girl used the "f" word. Out of the black came a bigger black that turned out to be Redonda, a thousand-foot tall rock of an island that belonged to no one and had no light, as it was uninhabited. I mean, Norway mined it for phosphate in the form of bird shit. Antigua claimed it for fishing rights and a man named Juan Carlos' poet father claimed it in the 1920s as no one had actually claimed it as yet, according to the newly formed World Court. This was followed by a dukedom awarded to Dr. Hunter S. Thompson, thus his nom du plume Raoul Dukes and his character of Duke in the cartoon strip Doonesbury, and a kingship claimed by an eccentric descendant of Charles the Bald, grandson of Charlemagne.

Turning the wheel just in the nick of time, we missed total destruction only to find ourselves caught up in the windless lee of the unclaimed, claimed, and reclaimed rock, with our sails aback. Waves were HUGE and crashing one hundred feet high on the cliffs so precariously close aboard that seawater was raining down upon us. Luckily the giant backwash is what saved us seafarers from doom as it washed us away from the cliffs and out into the wind line.

Fifty knots of wind now, and off we went again wanting for a sunrise so that we could see something. When we got a wee glimmer of light in the east I begin to think that it was better to be in the dark.

We were beating into huge seas accompanied with an extreme amount of wind. At first light we began to receive the first of the storm force squalls. You could see them coming all black in the sky and white on the ocean. When the first one hit us, I turned *Shadowfax* and ran with it, as any normal sailor would do in such an event. We took off down these waves at twenty knots of boat speed. Water was flying everywhere, and after one hour the squall abated and we turned to beat back upwind in a mere forty-five knots of breeze.

The only problem was that in the last hour we had sailed back toward Lenny for twenty miles and now had to sail three hours to gain the ground we had lost. This was not the way to go as on the radio we had been informed that this damn storm was still slowly moving in an east-southeast direction. As the next black and white squall approached I held on and weathered it out. We sailed into seventy knots of wind slamming to beat the band and now it was really wet. I was driving, my knees were shaking, and I told Dot that we should never be sailing into this kind of wind and sea but running with it. Yet running was taking us back toward the storm. Dot, bless her heart, reminded me that it might be blowing fifty or even seventy where we were now, but it was blowing 150 where we left...Kind of calms the nerves now don't it?

We passed boats all day, three that we never heard from again. Eight times I crossed a tug in tow with a barge. Out of the white he would appear slowly powering straight into the wind and sea. The spume would be flying over his bow and disappearing far to the stern of the barge. I chanced upon the captain of that tug a few months later who told me that my VMG (velocity made good) was 5.8 knots, for that was the speed he maintained throughout the entire storm. Not bad upwind speed for a catamaran in a hurricane was my response!

By mid-morning the National Hurricane Center Miami had a new prediction and projected Lenny to finally make its northerly turn and leave the area in the vicinity of Anguilla. It would seem that the storm had taken to meandering around as if looking for something or someone and decided that around St. Barth was not the place to find it. This was good news, for after eighteen hours of steering I was getting beat. We decided to seek safe harbor. Radio contact was made with Jolly Harbor, Antigua, but we were informed that waves in the channel were up to fifteen feet and entrance was impossible.

We tacked and headed toward the southeast corner of Guadeloupe and Des Heyse. Contacting a friend of mine there who was behind the new breakwater, we were informed that it too was out. Waves were breaking across the bay and the bay was seventy-five feet deep! They were continuing and crashing over the seawall. We tacked again and beat up the northwest coast of Guadeloupe, radioing the capitanerie at Port Louis. Same story: waves to twenty feet at the entrance, we were told.

All right then, I was thinking…*the northwest corner of the Saints will do.* The north coast must not have the swell as per usual and the little bay at Anse de Pont Pierre on the tiny French island between Guadeloupe and Dominica would do nicely for shelter. Beating over Cap Antigua we tacked again and beat on toward Cap Carpentier, the northeast point of the island. The tack carried us right into the center of the north coast of Guadeloupe and Le Moule, a tiny fishing village that

I knew, as I had been there before surfing, had a small harbor with a very strong dock to which I could lash *Shadowfax* alongside.

It was great as we approached. A flat sea, accompanied by forty knots of wind, was all that we had to endure. We were in the lee! Everything was backwards, but we were in the lee. I spied the harbor entrance and the channel marker. There was only one mile to go. I had been driving for twenty-two hours and the end was in sight. Until ominously the next black and white sea squall loomed on the horizon. Would we make it inside in time? Well, no, of course. The island, entrance, even the horizon, was blotted out by the wind and water. As I had been concentrating on finding the entrance to Le Moule, I had not paid attention to anything behind. Asking Dot if she happened to have seen another island she confided that she had indeed seen Antigua and gave me a compass bearing to its position. Ah, to sail with experienced sailors is such a relief.

The squall hit, I turned the boat, and we started another run at the storm; twenty-five knots this time and oddly enough on course to Antigua and quite safe, actually. *Shadowfax* loved the run. So I gave Dot the wheel and took a break. We covered the forty-five miles to Antigua in an hour and a half! I tried to sleep but was too pent up with energy to get my mind to shut down. Besides, Dot would just laugh with glee as that sixty-foot cat would jump on a wave and squirt ahead at twenty-five knots. The waves got bigger, the driver got happier, and the boat became more and more stable. What a ride!

As we neared the island, Dot relinquished the helm so that I could negotiate our landfall. At twenty knots of speed, Falmouth Harbor, Antigua, was coming up fast. I spied a mega yacht moored in the interior, but it was not until the last minute that I found the entrance to Falmouth. It was made apparent by a huge wave breaking entirely across the channel! Falmouth is a ship's harbor. The British fleet used to lie at anchor in there, and here we had fifteen-foot waves breaking across that deep-water entrance!

I looked behind me to turn the boat around only to see the next swell feathering on the top and beginning to break. There was no going back now. I was between two fifteen-foot breaking waves, so damn them damn torpedoes and full speed ahead, as some nut somewhere once said. We shot inside the harbor as that giant of a wave broke behind us. It caught up with us in the channel, picked up the "*Fax*," and shades of Luis in '95, we surfed it in! I could literally look to my side and see us riding what now was an eight-foot roller all the way through the anchorage. The wave broke all across Pigeon Beach, over the long dock, and continued around the headland with us still on it.

As I "kicked out" (a surfing term for getting out of a wave) the "Fax," our watery ride continued its long, winding break through the first floor of Falmouth Apartments! We coasted the catamaran head to wind and immediately got an anchor down. It was so relatively calm in there…blowing forty knots maximum as we settled back on our primary anchor. We felt saved!

My good friend, the yacht club marina owner, upon seeing us from his house come surfing into the harbor, came zooming out on his thirty-one-foot Intrepid motorboat. He, in all his zeal, promptly ran into the back of us, knocking a hole in the aft crossbeam and we sustained the only damage on the boat after twenty-four hours of sailing in a hurricane! I had to laugh. We were safe, we were alive, and we had the marina owner yelling that didn't we know there was a hurricane out there? "Of course we did," was my reply, "why do you think we are in here?!" But Lenny was not done yet.

Our meandering threat had decided not to exit stage right and leave the scene via Anguilla. Instead the thing took a bead on St. Kitts, my second home away from home, for who knows what devious reason. So we went to set up a storm moorage. But, just as on *Skyjack* in Hurricane Emily in '83 and on *El Tigre* in the storm of '84,Klaus, and *Shadowfax* with Luis in '95, there was so much water in the air that the outboard would not start. Therefore we sailed out a second storm anchor and hunkered for the blow.

It was now the evening of the eighteenth of November. Lenny had been smashing around the Lesser Antilles for twenty-four hours without respite, and we were snug as a bug inside Falmouth Harbor, Antigua. We tuned into Antigua Radio and listened to Joyle, the voice of gloom and doom. Although the National Hurricane Center Miami, The Met Office in St. Maarten, and Meteo France all had different models and predictions as to what Lenny would actually do, none of them included it going to Antigua. Well, Joyle thought different and we expected the worst. It blew forty-five knots all night and all the next day. Dot and I watched the few mono hulls in the harbor doing gunnels to gunnels rolls as we sat and had a romantic dinner including wine and champagne. You just gotta love those catamarans in a rolling, pitching anchorage. By near sunset on the nineteenth the wind quickly abated and we were able to launch our dinghy without it blowing away and went to shore, well, to the bar actually, and a piña colada!

Halfway from Falmouth to the Admiral's Inn at English Harbor, we ran across all the sailors that had been ashore for the past twelve hours heading BACK to their boats. You see, the barometer had, just like that, dropped to the bottom, a sure indicator that Joyle was correct and the storm was going to pay us a visit. But after forty-eight hours of sailing and weathering a blow I said screw that, we were off to the bar for a piña colada! Sucking that thing down at the bar in the AD Inn, I noticed a natural phenomenon only seen once by me in my charmed life, and that was three weeks earlier during Jose on St. Barth...The eye of a hurricane at sunset!

The bartender lady—and I really should remember her name—made a religious remark and had a look on her face like the second coming. "Lawd, Lawd, Lawd," she said, "wot in de Lawd's name is dat out deh?!" I promptly turned around and saw it too. It was the color...only two of them. The sky was lemon yellow. Not canary yellow, not orange yellow, but lemon yellow, and everything else was mauve...everything! I said to the lady, "What, lady, you never seen no sunset when the eye of a hurricane passes over?" Then I ordered two more piña coladas.

We, my friends, had just lucked out. The storm, you see, had exploded at sunset on the nineteenth and the eye became fifty-six miles across, putting Antigua in the center of it. Amazing thing to have happened and Joyle had called it. The wind quit, the birds came out to sing, and it was for Dee and me a very magical moment.

Quietly Lenny passed Antigua and continued on his east-southeast course. By the twentieth he had reformed, and by the twenty-third, six hundred nautical miles to the east, he stopped—and came back! But there is a God. At the end of that day, Lenny finally dissipated after his four-day hunt for who knows what. I did have a sneaking suspicion that "who knows what" would be me. But perhaps super-suspicion is the word to use here. Who knows, I was safe, Dot was safe, and the "*Fax*" was sound.

Dot and I packed up and headed back to St. Barth to help out in the clean-up and to see what damage had been heaped on the Rockefeller Estate. Being all bassackwards, instead of the typical run back in a southerly, we had a light beat through the narrows of St. Kitts. We motor sailed mostly and had to stop in the capital, Basse Terre, for gas. What a wreck that town was. They had just completed a huge cruise ship port to handle seven ships alongside at a time and it was all gone...GONE! The waves had destroyed all but the harbormaster's office. Just pilings were sticking up. The yachts and boats that were tucked away inside the inner harbor of the marina were on land, and the land was in the sea. But where were the giant concrete ships docks, the steel and concrete walkways, the massive breakwater, and the piers...all gone. I flashed instantly on the little pier we had just finished at the Rockefeller property so that big boats could land there. It was all concrete and rebar and sheet pile that had been pounded forty feet into the bottom, but it was tiny compared to this! And this was utterly destroyed. By the way, there was no gas dock.

The local fisherman who lived in the country spared me enough gasoline to get home, so off we went up the lee of St. Kitts. Well, what was usually the lee had been devastated by the surf and storm surge. Waves had been up to twenty-five feet, and the destruction made that evident. All the fishing villages along the water's edge were damaged or simply not there. Passing The Fortress at Brimstone Hill, I remembered that for the longest time there had been a lone tramp steamer left over from its smuggling days aground along the cliffs. Now there was nothing to show for its existence save the bow section and four fuel tanks along the rocky shore. A fifth tank had made it around the island and washed up on the beach at Grand Fond…in St. Barth! Motoring on we turned at Sandy Point, a long black sand beach marking the northwest end of St. Kitts. What point? I should say. There were still eight-foot waves now breaking through the trees! No sand, no point.

Upon arriving to St. Barth that evening, I went to the north side of the island and Baie du St. Jean. My mooring there was still in place. Driving my jeep over to Gustavia, I noticed light damage to home and roof. One yacht that had stayed was now half in, half out of the water beside the Rock Dock. The sea wall was gone and there were stones all across the road. Water in the garages had been about three feet above normal as there was sand and shell inside a refrigerator that was stored there. And the storm stories, they were something to hear.

Saba, the Dutch island that had lost its radio tower during David in '79, had lost its tower again. Its anemometer had registered 145 knots (like 166.75 mph!) before the tower went over. St. Maarten had recorded 27.5 inches of rain in twenty-four hours and twenty inches were recorded in St. Barth. Deaths were set at seventeen with three yachts missing. One had a survivor who, after the boat went down off the Dutch island of Statia, had donned a wet suit and grabbed a boogie board and floated until the storm blew him up on Orient Beach in St. Martin two days later!

In St. Barth, the wave height in the harbor had peaked at sixteen feet...in the harbor. A friend of mine, Nannard, had seen waves breaking over the islets of Gros Islet, and the islets are ten meters high. Luckily for St. Barth there is not much on the lee side of the island except for Shell Beach, which was gone, and the bay at Colombier and the estate dock of the Rockefellers.

My God, did that part of the island get it the worst. The waves had destroyed the new dock. The boats, the davits, the road were all gone. Sheet pile were scattered on the bottom for over a three hundred-yard area. The doors to the dock's garage and pump house were matchsticks. The new pier was in chunks and inside the pump house, and the truck was on top of it all. The overhead fluorescent lights were full of seawater. There was a strange boat in there too. The biggest piece was maybe six inches by six inches. It had no name or a number, just a lot of little bits of boat. The desalination plant seemed intact, yet the brine reservoir had sponges and seaweed in it! Remember the fifty-two full-grown coconut palms we had planted along the beach of the estate? Well, nine remained. The beach was not there, so how could the coconut grove survive?

What was left of the beach was not sand but seaweed, stone, sponges, corals, about a million baby conch, and, get this, twenty-two sets of snorkeling gear. Bare boaters must have for years been losing a fin or snorkel or two and, not having the gumption to dive them up, had left them for ole Davey Jones. I got them instead.

Just what happened to the estate house, you may wonder. Shit, was that a mess. As if the flood of Jose was not bad enough, Lenny and his eye must have packed a tornado or two because the damage was surreal. All of the bolts on the storm shutters had been ripped off and the shutters were strewn about the property. One of the shutters had gone THROUGH the 12mm plate glass window, and the wind following had taken everything in the TV room out one of the windows in the back, window frame and all. The huge cedar tree that was at the exit point in the garden had its largest limb twisted off like a weed and was not to be found. And true to tornado form, the only thing remaining in that room was my desk, the phone, my pen, and my address book still open to the page I had been looking at when I opted to bail from the house five days before! I had been looking up Dot's phone number.

The aftermath of Lenny in 1999: The huge swell created by the storm caused untold damage to the "protected" leeward side of the islands. St. Maarten's Simpson Bay, a cargo vessel beached beside the airport.

Chapter 18

Don't Worry, Hurricanes NEVER Turn South!

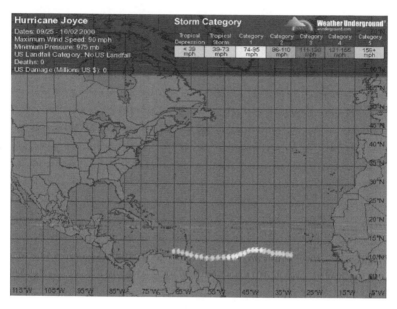

"JOYCE"
September 25–October 2, 2000

By the turn of the century I was sure hurricanes had it out for me and I had gotten quite used to running away from the storms. In 1999 I had ventured even out as far as Barbados, an island so far out in the Atlantic that it is not even mentioned in the cruising guides to the West Indies. For my summer haul out in 2000 I went again. They never get hurricanes out there and everyone speaks English...at least until they get liquored up, then that Bajan dialect is incomprehensible!

Busy—yes, that is his name—is quite the famous bajan businessman who had, in 1984, built the last Peter Spronk catamaran at the old yard at Landseair in St. Maarten. The cat was called *TIAMI,* an anachronism for "This Is A Moving Investment." The last of the sixty-foot Spronk cats to be built in the Caribbean and its crew of Busy, Noddie, and family, endeared me to themselves and Barbados. Busy had established a boatyard and haul-out spot just for catamarans and especially built for Spronk catamarans like *Shadowfax* on the island in Bridgetown, the capital.

The yard itself consisted of a workshop accompanied by a beautiful flat sandy beach, coconut trees for shade, and a trailer propelled by the Government Fisheries tractor was pushed into the sea under the floating cats, winched up tight to their bridge decks, and comfortably and quietly tugged up the beach across the exquisite white sand and under the cool of the shading palms. Next door to the left of the yard was a daytime cruise ship bar and to the right an all-night disco. I called this place the "Club Med of Haul-Out Spots." The haul-out fee to the fisheries was $50 bajan ($25 U.S.) and that was in and out. Plate lunch could be purchased across the street for $5 U.S., and because I was poor, Busy didn't charge me staying alongside his boatyard. Bliss and paradise; so what was the down side?

Well, it was Bridgetown, the capital of Barbados, and it was in the middle of the ghetto, so security could prove to be a problem. The locals all informed me and begged me to hire a security guard for the nighttime or else trouble would find me. But humph! I never had extra money for a guard. Shoots, by summer I was down to the last bit of cash saved for my annual haul-out, and a guard was not in the budget. I had always figured I should put all the money I made during charter season back into the boat. I would get it back out when I eventually sold the thing. As I have said before, in the Caribbean, Jah moves in strange ways, and it was no different here in Barbados.

Boatyard dogs are what came my way. The first day I ate at the plate lunch spot across the street, two of them, all scruffy and snaggle-toothed, came to pay me a visit. Giving them my leftovers endeared me to them and they to me just like stray dogs do. Fortunately for me they moved in, setting up camp right underneath *Shadowfax.* They seemed so cute during the day while I worked sanding, fixing, and painting the boat. They would wait calmly in the shade for lunch, pass by for a scratch and pet, and then return to a bit of slumber. But nighttime was a different story. The beasts were wild, growling, slavering animals. No one could get near that boat. Not even me! Well, almost: you see, every night I had to talk my way past the doggie guard post and up the ladder to beddy bye. And believe you me it took a lot of sweet talk to get past those two. No amount of dog food or chicken leg would do. Security guard, I say, who needs security guards?

It took three weeks to complete my annual haul-out and repairs on *Shadowfax*. Three lovely weeks with weekends surfing the east shore of Barbados or sailing radio-controlled sailboats with the world champion Peter "Rabbit" in a crater lake on top of the island. Rabbit, a long-time friend as well as a Spronk cat aficionado, was the man who had invited me to Barbados from the beginning of this adventure. He owned my old fifty-foot Spronk cat *Zwana*. His brother had Peter Spronk's personal boat *Pink Panther*, and his nephew had purchased and restored the famous sixty-foot Spronk cat *El Tigre* of hurricane stories past. His cousin had the fifty-foot *Rubiyacht*, an even older Spronk cat, and all the boats had been built in the same yard as Busy's *TIAMI*.

Because of the need for a dry dock facility in Barbados, Busy designed and built the trailer that carried the boats out of the water onto the Club Med-like beach and in turn had enticed me to this lovely island.

Jeez, from my description one would think Barbados would be a wonderful place to stay, and for the most I am sure that it is. However, for me...well, along came the storm. Joyce was her name. Doing the normal thing that Cape Verde storms do, Joyce started winding up far out in the Atlantic, but not so far as to escape our attention. Moving west at twelve to sixteen nautical miles per hour, she seemed to be staying pretty far south for a bit too long and we in Barbados started to worry.

The island, you see, had not had a storm touch them in the last fifty-four years, yet during hurricane season one always keeps a wary eye out to windward. And since hurricanes ALWAYS attempt to make a slight turn to the northwest, the seemingly below normal track was a bit worrying. Becoming a tropical storm on the twenty-fifth, I waited ashore in my paradisal leisure two more days to see what would ensue. On the twenty-sixth, Joyce was still in the eleven degree north latitude, well below us at thirteen degrees on Barbados. Note: there are sixty nautical miles to a degree. However on the twenty-seventh, Joyce was declared a hurricane and at the latitude of 12.5 degrees north and, moving in a now west-northwesterly direction, became a direct threat to Barbados. Having that sneaking suspicion that something was following me around, and with the local Bajans being superstitious as well, I decided it was time to make a plan!

The storm still being three to four days out gave us time to plan. First of all, Barbados has no natural port or hurricane holes (small, natural bays or harbor-like niches where a few boats could safely tie up). All the boats would have to be put on land. To do this, the government supplied a crane behind the breakwater of the deepwater cargo port to pull out most of the cats. The trailer of Busy's should have been available, but I was on it. Now me having survived way too many hurricanes already made me not want to be in another one, and so I opted to launch *Shadowfax*, freeing up the trailer for Busy's boat and allowing me to run away, run away!!! But I had no crew, and running away meant sailing south two days to Trinidad. I needed crew. Rabbit to the rescue was the bajan way and her name was Kendra.

She was Rabbit's crew on *Zwana,, aka Stiletto II,* a black bajan beauty and avid sailor to boot. It was just like a bajan to be helpful, but to make one look good at the same time was a bonus. We provisioned the boat and launched on the morning of the twenty-ninth. No looking back at that beautiful beach abode now, it was off to Trinidad and in a hurry, for the morning position of Joyce had her going south once again at 11.5 degrees latitude or between us and Trinidad and getting stronger. Once again moving westward, the storm was now a threat not only to Barbados but also to the Antilles anywhere from Grenada to St. Lucia. We had to get south.

It is 182 nautical miles from Barbados to Trinidad. You have to skirt the southwest side of Tobago and go into a cut between the big island and another one that housed the leprosy colony in days gone by. Now sailing, that should be about an all day, all night voyage in West Indian time reference. Leaving on the morning of the twenty-ninth, then all day all night should have put us off Trinidad by the morning of the thirtieth. But no, there was no wind. There was a hurricane approaching and it took all the wind.

Unfortunately after twenty-four hours of sailing, we were nowhere near Trinidad but rather off the southwestern tip of Tobago. Joyce was threatening, according to the radio, having dipped farther south than any hurricane I had ever heard of. I mean, what hurricane goes south? It was as if Joyce was…no. I won't say it… Ok, I will…following me. We considered Tobago as a stopping place, but the only bay I was familiar with was Mt. Irving, a GREAT surf spot but not a place one would weather a storm. Besides, this storm had to turn north. Hurricanes NEVER go to Trinidad.

Tobago was not the place to hole up, so on to Trinidad a-motor sailing we went. Another all day and with little gas left and variable winds we neared the island. It looked like landfall would be near sunset with maybe a half a gallon of gas to spare. Luckily for us, I thought, was that the hurricane hole for Charimungus, known as Scotland Bay, lies right after you pass through the cut, and in we went near sunset to a tight bay full of boats. But heck, I was in a catamaran, right. Drawing eighteen inches of water with the boards up we went through the fleet and onto the beach, placing two anchors at sixty degrees off the bow and backing up, only to drag the two anchors together, raking the bottom clean of debris. Rugs, rags, a bicycle, balls of fishing line, fish traps, large cans, you name it; we raked it…far into the night, for four hours, and never set a hook! We would get a semi hook then full power in reverse to make sure we were set, and lo and behold, junk, junk, and more junk. We were in the shit, to say the least. Joyce, at last reports, was bearing down on Trinidad, due to hit in a few hours, and we didn't even have an anchor set yet. Night had fallen and I was both frustrated and tired. Plan B had to be implemented.

One should always have a Plan B and I, upon arriving in this newfound place, had checked the chart for a second anchorage should the first one fail. It was across the cut in a smaller bay surrounded by homes. Morris Bay was its name and pulling in and anchoring in the dark was no easy feat, and we hoped for the center of the bay as our optimal mooring spot. Using the lights of the surrounding abodes as a guide, we placed *Shadowfax* mid-bay-ish and, finding ok holding, deployed our three anchors in a storm array. By eleven p.m. we were settled in and waited for the approaching storm. Trinidad was under storm warnings and the center had now continued its southerly trek from 10.5 degrees north to 10.3 degrees. We were in the bull's eye.

Sitting awake all night with the radio on is easy when you are under stress. Drink plenty of coffee, eat munchies, step out the deckhouse to test the wind, and wait. But nothing happened. No maydays on the radio, no shrieking winds, no rain, nothing. When first light came, the size of Morris Bay showed us that if Joyce had passed we would have been in somebody's living room. The eight o'clock weather report had the storm abated and whatever was left of the center passing very near Tobago and then on to the southwest of Grenada.

Amazing, incredible, and OMG, I thought. I had seen the shear on the tops of the approaching clouds at sunset as we neared Trinidad but had no idea that the shear would blow the storm out. Weaken it, maybe, but not completely dissipate the storm. "Unpredictable" is the word they use to describe these things and that is what we got, thank You very much. I just survived the shortest-lived hurricane in my life.

Up the anchors and off to Charimungus was the call of the day on the first of October using our last teaspoonful of fuel and a fair current. And there we found an oil spill, no hurricane damage, but oil among us. I called the port from then on "Oil Amongus." What a mess, but at least no damage to the island, no loss of life.

After anchoring, we launched the dinghy onto a black sheen and zoomed ashore to the fuel dock to replenish our supply. No dollars, but a credit card near max limit worked to fill twenty gallons of jury jugs and let us spend enough time on the fuel dock to see Shadowfax dragging anchor at a nice clip and heading for the beach! I leapt into the dinghy with a jug of gasoline, leaving Kendra holding the smoking credit card waiting for the receipt, and flew out to the boat. Sailors in two dinghies from neighboring yachts had already showed up trying to stop the boat from hitting the beach as I scrambled aboard to start the motor. Before I could get gas in and the motor started, she came to an abrupt stop, the anchor hooked up on something under all of that oil and stopped the boat with the rudder inches from the bottom of the muddled bay. After not sailing in a hurricane, not sailing through someone's living room, and not sailing onto the beach in "Oil Amongus," I just knew that Shadowfax had an angel somewhere.

What a scene, this Trinidad, truly a mess! By now all I wanted to do was to get out of there before I had too much oil on the hulls. But I had to go through customs first. That part was a breeze and those Trinny customs guys were great. Then it was off to provision and then to the marine store to get some odds and ends a boat always needs after a passage. We got all that completed by early afternoon, and even though there was very little wind left after Joyce had passed, we opted to motor around to the northwest bay of the island…La Vache Bay…and anchor for the night. All we had to do was to get up the anchor and go. Well, that anchor was stuck and stuck good. I mean, dive up good. There was no power-it-up or back-it-down or nothing…it was stuck, dive up stuck, and the water was covered with oil! I gave Kendra the helm and donned mask, snorkel, and fins and reluctantly went over the side.

Using the anchor rode as a guide, I pulled myself down through the black water. The oil seemed to be about one foot thick, yet after about five feet of depth the water became very clear. I could plainly see the anchor wedged in an old shipwreck in about twenty feet of water. Not wanting to resurface and re-oil my fouled body, I continued to the bottom and yanked the anchor loose from its entangling debris. I then shot to the surface, quickly swimming back to *Shadowfax,* into the dinghy, and then on board, leaving a trail of black oil. Then it was off for an exit of the harbor instead of heading again to the beach.

The question was what to do with the slick of spilled oil now coating my body from head to toe. I looked like a survivor from the sinking of the battleship *Arizona.* Ruining one towel, I searched around me for some kind of solvent as Kendra came to the rescue. Going into the galley she grabbed a full roll of paper towels and, on the way past the tool room, grabbed a large can of WD40. That stuff is the miracle worker! Slick and clean was how I turned out as we got under way. Barbados bound and 182 nautical miles of no wind or light wind on the nose. We motored to La Vache Bay.

What a way to start an after hurricane adventure home. The bay is sixty feet deep right up onto the shore. There is a small, sandy beach, an old ruin of a mansion at the base of the cliff, and a fisherman named Frank McCee between the only place and ourselves to put out an anchor...on that beach. We worked our way in, set a stern anchor as we neared the beach, and then working around the fisherman's net, we set the main anchor out on the beach and backed up. Expecting the fisherman to give us some grump as they do in some islands, I waved, gave a smile, and invited him over. What a nice guy ole Frank was. Not only did he offer us fish, he offered us dinner at his house, the ruin on the beach, where he had everything except power and ice. Running water? That was no problem; there was a stream from a waterfall running through the place! Ice? Now that was a problem. It seems he had to go by bus to get it and the bus stop was a forty-five-minute walk out of the jungle to the road. So when he offered us ice, I respectfully declined.

It was a wonderful evening, and by morning we were kind of slow to leave. I don't remember if it was the company, the fresh fish and vegetables, or the fifteen-year-old Trinidad rum…or even just the hospitality, but we certainly didn't just jet out of there. But off to Barbados it was on a beautiful clear day, calm sea, and unfortunately, a light breeze on the nose. On a port tack we were headed for the mid-Atlantic, and on a starboard tack we might clear the island of Carriacou, just north of Grenada. I chose the latter one, in the event we needed to stop again for gas.

We sailed, well, motor-sailed, really, off into light and shifting wind conditions. The current was against us as well as the wind. But it was a beautiful day, I had survived another hurricane, and we caught fish! By four in the afternoon, sailing from four to eight knots, we hooked two mahi mahi, the fish so good they named it twice. I filleted them buggers for dinner, and as Kendra prepared the evening meal, I set the autopilot to task and went forward on the net to enjoy the ride. And the dolphins came, about twenty of them, to play under the net and between the hulls of *Shadowfax*. Two of them in particular, one with a pink belly another with a damaged fin, came quite close to the bows time and time again. I went farther forward stretching myself out on the deck above the bows and held my arms out as if I were flying. Dang if those two dolphins didn't come by, jump out of the water, and touch my outstretched hands! Not once or twice but numerous times they came by…High-fives from the dolphins. It was a magic moment few sailors encounter. I was appreciative. Kendra didn't believe me.

By dark and dinner the weather began to change with squalls off Grenada. Hand steering through a dark and rainy night got us past the island of Grenada and under the island of Carriacou, but we would probably have to sail upwind until the weather improved, the wind shifted, or both. I wanted to stop in Tyrell Bay. That was what we did. "Black" was the word to describe the night. Even through my Steiner binoculars it was black. I spied a tiny shipboard light in the bay, and my GPS got me there safely. A barking dog held me up and I anchored just behind the sound. There was ample water indicated on the depth sounder, so down the oily anchor went. Safe and sound sat the "*Fax.*"

First light woke the dog and in turn the dog woke me. Lo and behold I was anchored right behind THE *Mermaid of Carriacou!* John Smith, the romantically infamous captain, author, diver, fisherman, lifesaver, and shipwright had not only Bianca the parrot but also a little rootin' tootin' watchdog. Nice homecoming we had. Wanting to celebrate my good fortune, I went ashore to get incitements only to find out that in Trinidad the buggers had charged my trinny dollar bills to my credit card in U.S. dollars, a difference of about five to one. My thin banking account was not only wiped out, I was in arrears. The card was fried. Gloomily returning to the boat, I checked the change can and found 52 EC (Eastern Caribbean) dollar coins. Asking John what I could buy with that, he beamed, "ICE, you can buy ice, for I, me son, has the beer!"

John, it seemed, had helped a fellow in and out of the mangroves in Tyrell Bay to weather the passing Joyce and had been rewarded with a case of beer, warm, but beer anyway. We had a nice day aboard the ole *Mermaid.* John cooked up the second mahi and entertained

Kendra with true and eloquent stories of the *Mermaid*, himself, and hurricanes. We laughed and drank all the damn day. It's always good to run across Cap'n John!

By evening the weather turned nice, the wind shifted a little, and Kendra and I opted to head out for Barbados. The first long tack took us to the leeward side of St.Vincent. Skirting the Grenadines to port, we gently cruised the entire evening. Tacking under a starry sky, we finally got the boat headed to Barbados. Changing course about twenty times as the wind shifted, we worked our way far out into the Atlantic until by morning we could see the faint shadow of the island. By afternoon it was light squalls, rainbows, and favorable wind shifts so that by eight in the evening we arrived, anchored, and breathed a sign of relief and satisfaction. Kendra's trip was done. She was home after quite the adventure for an island girl, and I was in a jonesing state to get back to St. Barth.

Leaving Barbados is not an easy thing to do. The hospitality of those people is legendary, but three days later I was off. I had singlehanded many a boat, even once qualifying on a thirty-two-foot trimaran to sail in the OSTAR, the singlehanded transatlantic race. It takes special training to sleep for twenty minutes when one is tired. But that's how you do it because it takes a ship twenty minutes to go from horizon to horizon. You do not want one of them to run you down while you are taking a beauty nap!

So that was how I planned it. Sailing out of Bridgetown after many goodbyes and plenty of provision and rum for the trip home (Barbados is full of provision and rum), I made it as far as the northwest tip of the island before I had to stop. You see, it wasn't the rum that slowed me, it was the surf, and the surf was GOING OFF. I anchored Shadowfax up behind the point around which was the famous surf spot called Duppies. The name has something to do with ghosts, but what, I don't have the slightest idea. But I showed up like one. No one ever arrives by dinghy to Duppies. But here came Randy out of nowhere, slung out a little anchor, and paddled over into the line-up with the boys saying, "Now just where did he come from?" I adhered to the old adage "Seven waves or an hour, whichever comes first," had my fun, and spirited myself around the corner to be once again homeward bound and very content.

It was a beautiful sail home; it was just my autopilot and I. A tuna was caught and sushi was prepared. I just love to eat sushi. Water chuckled along the hull as the "*Fax*" made way in the light easterly winds, but the boat loved it and sailed nimbly along. I held my twenty-minute catnaps when tired yet never saw a ship. I used a tiny wind-up alarm clock with its ring-a-ding bell to wake me up set at twenty-minute intervals when needed. The night sky was as you read about with shooting stars, a moon, passing satellites, and the stars, all the stars. Morning came as I passed Martinique, then Dominica, and on toward Guadeloupe. The decision had to be made to go either around Marie Gallant or between it and Desirade. I chose the inside route under the larger island of Marie Gallant.

There, after dodging fish traps on the banks, I let my guard down. Tired after no real sleep but clear of obstacles for another fifty miles or so until I reached Antigua and also being out of the shipping lanes, I took a nap. It was a wonderful, dream-filled nap of a blissful hour and a half. I was shaken from my reverie by a low throbbing sound and as I opened my weary eyes, I noticed a HUGE cargo ship slipping by not five hundred FEET away! I didn't sleep after that till I was on my mooring in St. Barth!

Luckily it isn't that far a sail from Antigua to St. Barth, and in ten hours I was home. Sun up and St. Barth. You cannot beat that. My St. Barth friends were in wonderment at my storm story, for whoever heard of a hurricane going south? I definitely had made a name and legend out of these dang storms following me around, and after so long and so many storms I had started believing the rumors myself. But heh, the hurricane season was over. My saviors and secret agents in St. Barth, Sol and Charlie, had a day charter waiting for me and voila! I was back in the saddle again. There were euros in the pocket and no worries until next June.

The sixty-foot Spronk cat Shadowfax *sailing into Gustavia Harbor, 2000.*

Chapter 19

And There Never Was a Storm Again

The end of the millennium and I settled into my last charter season. We shot a movie, *Pickled,* for Quiksilver and the pro surfers of their team. After that the *"Fax"* was let out as a mother ship for Carlo Falcone's race boat and I competed in the Caribbean circuit with him and his crew. I fell in love and got left at the altar as the bride-to-be cancelled the event one week before the wedding. Everyone had a great party anyway. Life does have its ups and downs.

I sold *Shadowfax* before the beginning of the next hurricane season in June, and for some reason the storms couldn't find me and I have never been in a hurricane again…at least not up till now and it is 2010. But one never knows. I have since continued sailing and have survived storms at sea and been an anchor for my crew as I can truly confide in them as the shit hits the fan…"Ah, this is nothing!"

But during hurricane season from June 1 until November 30, every morning I check the National Hurricane Center Miami on the Internet and pray not to get a storm. I also pray for those that do. I do this because now, when I sit humbly aboard in a marina at night and the wind whistles through the rigging…it just doesn't have that same joyful sound it used to in my youth.

The End   I Hope

An Invocation to the Angel Zamiel:

In the name of the all-powerful Creator,
I invoke you, great Angel Zamiel,
As the Angel of hurricanes,
To calm the fury of this terrible storm;
May you divert its path from the most vulnerable
places
To blow itself out where few can come to harm.
I honor and thank you for hearing my prayer,
In the name of the Almighty.
Amen

From the Apocrypha

Made in the USA
San Bernardino, CA
12 December 2013